FOREWORD

After nearly a quarter century in radio and television broadcasting, I have come to admire and appreciate gifted ghost writers who help me deliver solid material that is fresh and stimulating. Even more rare is a writer who is able to make me think that I'm reading my very own words. Karl Haffner is one of those gifted wordsmiths.

It has been my privilege to work with Karl Haffner on a number of projects. A prophecy seminar, Adventist Healthcare Mission conferences, charity golf tournaments, board meetings, Sabbath School classes, hospital committees, church services, strategic planning sessions, and this book—all have been joint efforts with Karl. Much of the content for this book originated as scripts that I had the joy of helping to shape and share as broadcasts for the *Voice of Prophecy* radio program during 2006 (1 Peter) and 2008 (2 Peter).

Back then, of course, I had no idea that I would have the good fortune of later working closely with Karl in Ohio. These days I am thrilled to be able to collaborate with Karl on many projects. I find his spiritual insights to be most illuminating. His joy is infectious. And his unwavering commitment to sharing the message of living hope so prevalent in the epistles of Peter is inspiring.

I highly recommend this book. I pray that in this spiritual journey, your faith "may be proved genuine and may result in praise, glory and honor when Jesus Christ is revealed" (1 Peter 1:7).

Lonnie Melashenko

CONTENTS

SECTION 2: 2 PETER: KEEP ON, CHRISTIANS

SECTION 1

1 PETER: WHAT'S IT ALL ABOUT?

Chapter 1

SURVIVAL

---

1 Peter 1:1–12

The *U.S. Government Peace Corps Manual* for volunteers details what to do if an anaconda attacks you.

Related to the boa constrictor, the anaconda is the largest snake species in the world. It grows to thirty-five feet in length and weighs 300 to 400 pounds.

1. If you are attacked by an anaconda, do not run. The snake is faster than you are.
2. Lie flat on the ground. Put your arms tight against your sides, your legs tight against one another.
3. Tuck your chin in.
4. The snake will begin to nudge and climb over your body.
5. Do not panic.
6. After the snake has examined you, it will begin to swallow you from the feet end—always from the feet end. Permit the snake to swallow your feet and ankles. Do not panic!
7. The snake will now begin to suck your legs into its body. You must lie perfectly still. This will take a long time.
8. When the snake has reached your knees, slowly and with as little movement as possible, reach down, take your knife, and very gently slide it into the side of the snake's

CAUGHT BETWEEN TWO WORLDS

mouth between the edge of its mouth and your leg, then
suddenly rip upwards, severing the snake's head.
9. Be sure you have your knife.
10. Be sure your knife is sharp.[1]

You may want to tear out this page and keep it handy for the next time an anaconda starts nibbling up your legs. (For the record, Snopes.com claims the "anaconda defense" is false; so if it doesn't work for you, well, you can't sue me.) On second thought, just hang on to the entire book. You may not need it for a snake bite, but it will come in handy when you are attacked by the devil who "prowls around like a roaring lion looking for someone to devour" (1 Peter 5:8). For physical and spiritual threats alike, it's important be vigilant if you want to survive.

The apostle Peter offers timely counsel for survival. His letters offered hope to Christians who were threatened both physically and spiritually. Before we consider the apostle's advice, however, it's helpful to get context with a crash course in Roman history.

HISTORICAL CONTEXT

Perhaps you've heard the phrase "Nero fiddled while Rome burned." Some historians believe that this saying can be traced to July 19, A.D. 64, when Rome was torched by an arsonist.

It was common knowledge in that day that Nero disliked Rome's architectural layout. The inner-city streets were too narrow; the buildings were dilapidated. When foreign dignitaries came to visit Rome, Nero was embarrassed to give them a tour of his city.

So Nero constructed a model of an improved, symmetrical Rome. But Nero knew that his ambition would never be realized—unless, of course, by some stroke of fate the old city would be destroyed. So it has been suggested that this demented Roman emperor coaxed fate along and set his city ablaze.

Following the fire, incensed Roman citizens rallied against Nero, demanding retribution. Feeling the heat, Nero claimed, "The Christians did it. They have destroyed our beloved city in hopes of building another city for themselves." He then commanded, "Soldiers, arrest all Christians and throw them in a dungeon."

In their commentary on 1 Peter, Pastor Doug Murren and Barb Shurin explain, "Having his soldiers arrest the Christians en masse at their meeting places, Nero not only lent credence to his monstrous lie, but also cleverly and diabolically got the Roman senators and citizens off his back. This marked the beginning of the Christians' hiding and meeting in the cata-combs under the city—the approximate time when 1 Peter was written."[2]

It was a time of severe persecution when Christians were fed to half-starved lions for sport. Christians struggled to survive. To encourage these Christians, Peter penned two letters that resound with hope.

GREETING

The first letter begins with this salutation,

> Peter, an apostle of Jesus Christ,
> To God's elect, strangers in the world, scattered throughout Pon-tus, Galatia, Cappadocia, Asia and Bithynia, who have been chosen according to the foreknowledge of God the Father, through the sanc-tifying work of the Spirit (1:1, 2).

There's something warm about this introduction, isn't there? Peter writes to God's people scattered throughout Asia Minor and reminds them that they have been chosen. William Barclay comments, "Surely there can be no greater compliment and privilege in all the world than to be chosen by God."[3] Who doesn't like to be chosen?

God has chosen you and me, but for what? Peter answers, "for obedience to Jesus Christ and sprinkling by his blood: Grace and peace be yours in abundance" (verse 2). God has chosen us for obedience. The apostle does not mince with words in his challenge for us to commit to radical obedi-ence. He calls us to grow into the likeness of Christ.

A. E. Housman captured the odd irony of being chosen by God and yet failing to obey Christ's command to accept all people as God's "chosen." Listen to his pithy poem,

> How odd
> Of God
> To choose
> The Jews.
> To which it has been added:
> But not so odd
> As those who choose
> The Jewish God

And spurn the Jews.[4]

We are chosen for obedience. Thus, we must obey *all* God's commands—including His call to love all people.

Following his introduction, Peter begins with this doxology in verse 3, "Praise be to the God and Father of our Lord Jesus Christ!"

SURVIVAL MATTERS

Next, Peter begins his message. Keep in mind who would be reading this letter. Picture the dispersed Christians who are being hunted. Imagine Sister Martha or Brother Nicodemus holed up in some hovel with other believers. In all likelihood, each person was staring down death.

When your life is threatened, you don't talk about trivial matters. You concentrate on what *really* matters. As we would expect, Peter does just that. He talks about life-and-death stuff.

Peter's letter reads like the spiritual equivalent to the book series *The Worst-Case Scenario Survival Handbook*. Joshua Piven and David Borgenicht have struck gold with this series. With more than four million copies sold worldwide, the survival series has a cultlike following.

Each book is a manual, written in a factual tone, based on interviews with experts in a variety of fields. The chapters offer instructions on how to survive any imaginable situation. For example, if your parachute fails to open, you're supposed to "signal to a jumping companion"—but the book doesn't say what to do if you're jumping alone! In case you're attacked by an alligator, you need to go for the gator's eyes and nose. OK? Now you know.

The authors say in the preface, "The principle behind this book is a simple one: You just never know. You never really know what life will throw at you, what is sitting around the corner. You never really know when you might be called upon to choose life or death with your actions. But when you are called, you need to know what to do. That's why this book is written."[5]

Peter could have used the same preface in his book, for this letter is a survival guide to Christians. Maybe you need a survival guide right now. You're trying to survive an illness, you have an unrelenting work schedule, or you're struggling to survive an abusive relationship.

If you're fighting to survive, take heart. Peter offers a handbook with some helpful counsel to saints striving to be survivors. You might think of this opening passage as three chapters in *Peter's Survival Handbook*.

1. YOU WILL OUTLIVE ANY PROBLEM YOU FACE.

The first chapter reminds us of this truth: *You will outlive any problem you face.* Beginning in verse 3, Peter writes,

> In his great mercy he has given us new birth into a living hope through the resurrection of Jesus Christ from the dead, and into an inheritance that can never perish, spoil or fade—kept in heaven for you, who through faith are shielded by God's power until the coming of the salvation that is ready to be revealed in the last time. In this you greatly rejoice, though now for a little while you may have had to suffer grief in all kinds of trials (verses 3–6).

Peter provides a wonderful perspective to Christians who are struggling to survive. He reminds us of our living hope in the resurrected Christ. "Your salvation is coming," Peter reminds us. "Rejoice, though now for a little while you may have had to suffer grief in all kinds of trials" (verse 6).

Whatever problem you're facing, if you accept Christ as your resurrected Savior, you will outlive your problem. It is in this hope that we see beyond the anguish of our world.

It's an old story, but worth repeating. Around the turn of the twentieth century, a missionary couple was returning home on a ship after serving for twenty-five years in Africa. On board was a famous passenger, Theodore Roosevelt, who was returning from an African safari. Since Roosevelt was a candidate for president, there were bands and crowds and much cheering as he stepped off the ship. The missionary remarked, "Isn't it amazing that he returns home after hunting a few weeks to bands and cheering crowds and all that adulation. But we return home from twenty-five years of serving God, and there's no one here even to greet us."

His wife tugged at his arm, smiled, and said, "But, dear, we're not home yet."[6]

That's worth remembering the next time you're wondering whether or not you can survive. Whatever problem you face, anchor your life in the living hope, our resurrected Savior, Jesus Christ. You will outlive every heartache, every challenge, every tear.

In his book *Our Greatest Gift*, Henri Nouwen imagines twins—a brother and a sister—talking to each other in their mother's womb,

The sister said to the brother, "I believe there is life after birth."

The brother protested, "No, no, this is all there is. This is a dark and cozy place, and we have nothing else to do but to cling to the cord that feeds us."

The girl insisted, "There must be something more than this dark place. There must be something else, a place with light where there is freedom to move." Then she added, "And I think there is a mother."

"A mother!" the boy scoffed. "I have never seen a mother, and neither have you. Who put that idea in your head? As I told you, this place is all we have. This is not such a bad place, after all."

"But don't you feel these squeezes every once in a while? They're quite unpleasant and sometimes even painful."

"Yes," he answered.

"Well," the sister said, "I think that these squeezes are there to get us ready for another place, much more beautiful than this, where we will see our mother face-to-face."[7]

Don't think for a moment that this dark world is all there is! The day is coming when you will see your Maker face-to-face. Any "squeeze" you're feeling now is temporary; you *will* outlive it.

2. YOUR FAITH IS REFINED IN HARDSHIP.

Next, Peter continues his encouragement to persecuted Christians by saying, *"Your faith is refined in hardship."* He writes, "[Your trials] have come so that your faith—of greater worth than gold, which perishes even though refined by fire—may be proved genuine and may result in praise, glory and honor when Jesus Christ is revealed" (verse 7).

The Bible teaches that our faith is refined by the fires we endure. This verse has become especially meaningful to me during the past year. On September 8, 2008, our church school, Spring Valley Academy, caught fire in the electrical room—causing millions of dollars of damage. Thankfully no one was injured. But for the remaining 2008–2009 school year, we held classes in a vacant building some eight miles from our campus. It was more than a little inconvenient.

The damage was extensive. The fire even forced us to delay the 2009 school year by a week. But what a day of rejoicing it was when we were back in our building. The local paper reported,

> The gym is still closed, and some of the new office furniture hasn't arrived, but Spring Valley Academy will again host students, who

spent nearly a year in another school building after a[n] electrical fire. . . .

Those affiliated with the school who completed the 2008-09 school year at the former Ridgeville Christian School say they are relieved to re-enter the 41-year-old building that has housed the tight-knit school and its community.

"We can't believe it," said Vicki Swetnam, the school's recruiting and marketing manager. "We're all pinching ourselves. . . .

"In spite of the fire, there has been a blessing," Swetnam said. "We've returned to an improved facility."[8]

Nearly the entire building was gutted, and the result is that now we have a brand-new school building! While we would have never wished for this trial, board members, parents, staff, and students alike agree that much good has come out of the flames. Our faith has been strengthened. Our characters have been refined. Our God has proven faithful.

Peter reminds us that fires can refine us as a people of faith. In the words of actress Brittany Murphy, "Everybody has difficult years, but a lot of times the difficult years end up being the greatest years of your whole entire life, if you survive them."[9]

Our faith is refined by fire. It was true for Spring Valley Academy. It was true for Shadrach, Meshach, and Abednego. It was true for Gilbert Tuhabonye (*Too-ha-bon-yay*).

Gilbert's journey began in the war-torn country of Burundi. Today he lives in Austin, Texas. His is an inspiring story of survival.

In 1993, Gilbert lay buried under a mound of smoldering bodies. He was a teenager, caught in the crossfire of the centuries-old battle between the Hutu and Tutsi tribes. Fueled by deep hate, the Hutu students at Kibimba high school, joined by their parents and other Hutu tribesmen, forced more than one hundred Tutsi children and teachers into a small room and tormented them with machetes. Both the survivors and the dead were torched with fire. The Hutus then partied and taunted their victims for the next nine hours.

Gilbert shielded himself from the fire with the bodies of his classmates. After hours of inconceivable pain, twice having tried to take his own life, Gilbert heard a voice within say, "You don't want to die." With his back and legs on fire, he used a charred bone to break through one of the windows. On scorched feet, Gilbert jumped free of the fire and ran into the cover of the night—the lone survivor of one of the most horrific massacres in the long, bloody history of the Hutu-Tutsi war.

Today, Gilbert is on a mission: to show others what one man—set on fire and left for dead—can accomplish. His very name hints at his divine calling in life. *Tuhabonye* means "a son of God."

"In Burundi," Gilbert explains, "your last name has to have meaning. When I was born, it was a difficult time. It was right after the war. There had been a big drought, crickets attacked the crops—and then my mother broke her ankle. When I was born, she said, 'This is not my son. This is a son of God.' "

When Gilbert's mom visited him in the hospital (where he remained for three months after his narrow escape from the genocide), she said to him, "If it wasn't for God, you are dead."

Gilbert has struggled with that notion. He wonders, *What about the others? They, too, were valued children of God. Why weren't they spared?* Gilbert explains, "That's the thing I didn't understand. Afterward, I asked myself, 'Why me? Why did I survive?' "

Gilbert answers by saying, "Eventually, I realized I had to help people, coaching them, telling them my story, telling what happened. When I help people, I feel good."

Gilbert's story in *Reader's Digest* concludes with this summary, "He's a flesh-and-blood symbol, a real-life survivor, a true son of God, a man on a mission."[10]

His remarkable story of survival serves as an inspiration to millions. After all, everybody faces harsh challenges, right? Who is immune to disappointment and pain? The real question is this: How can we survive the inevitable flames in life?

3. GOD IS AT WORK EVEN WHEN YOU CAN'T SEE HIM.

Peter answers by saying, *"You will outlive any problem you face. Your faith is refined in hardship. And finally, God is at work even when you can't see Him."*

Listen to Peter, "Though you have not seen him, you love him; and even though you do not see him now, you believe in him and are filled with an inexpressible and glorious joy, for you are receiving the goal of your faith, the salvation of your souls" (verses 8, 9).

Even though you cannot see God in the darkness of this world, He is at work. In his book, *The Dance of Hope,* Bill Frye tells the story of a blind student at the University of Colorado. The student lost his sight as a teenager during an explosion in his garage. But the accident not only stole his sight, it raped him of his hope. He became an angry and embittered young man.

The boy recounts, "I retreated to my bedroom and wouldn't even come out for meals. For months, I wouldn't speak to anybody. I resolved to live the rest of my life in misery."

Finally the young man's father had had enough. "Son," he said, "enough of this pity party. Get on with your life. Winter's coming and I need you to install the storm windows."

The boy protested, "But how can I install storm windows? I'm blind!"

The father replied, "Find a way. Do it before I get home from work tonight." The boy heard the door slam as his father left. He scowled, "OK, I'll show him! He'll be sorry when I fall off the ladder and break my neck."

Groping through the garage, he found the windows and the ladder. Cautiously, he went to work. To his surprise, he successfully installed all of them. By day's end, the father's desire was fulfilled. The boy performed his first constructive work since the accident. That simple act boosted his courage to take on another project, and then another, until he got his life back.

Then the young man shared the rest of his story, "It was a year later that I learned that as I was installing those windows my father was never more than four feet from me the entire day."

You see, the father was not about to abandon his boy. Your heavenly Father feels the same way about you. Peter tells us, "God is keeping careful watch over us" (1 Peter 1:5, *The Message*).

A FINAL SURVIVAL STORY

Friend, I don't know your survival story, but I know this: If you claim Jesus as your Savior, you will outlive any problem you face. Your faith will be refined through hardship. And God will always be with you—even when you can't see Him.

The survival story of Stephanie Fast illustrates all three of these principles. In her native South Korea, Stephanie was called a *toogie,* or a "foreign devil"—a child born of a Korean mother and an American father during the Korean War.

Abandoned at the age of four, she lived with gangs on the streets of Daejon, where she was abused emotionally, physically, and sexually. By the age of six, she had learned not to cry. Stephanie says, "You don't let people know you hurt because the more you let them know you hurt, the more pleasure it gives them. By the time I was six, I was dead emotionally."

Stephanie was persecuted, tortured, and finally discarded to die in a garbage dump. But she was miraculously rescued by a nurse employed by World Vision.

A few years later, a childless missionary couple, the Merwins, visited that World Vision orphanage and met Stephanie. She was covered with boils and dirt, lice-infected, worm-ridden, and cross-eyed from malnutrition. She was so dead emotionally that she rejected any gestures of compassion. But the Merwins sensed God speaking to their hearts, "She is the one for you."

So they adopted Stephanie.

Despite the healing love the Merwins poured into her, Stephanie's past tormented her throughout her teens. But as an adult she experienced a deeply personal encounter with Jesus. She realized that she could exchange her pain with Jesus at the cross. Finally she found her identity and purpose in the light of God's love.

Now Stephanie shares her riveting story of survival with audiences around the world. At the heart of her talk is this message, "There is no event in my life that I would be better without."[11]

Stephanie offers a compelling snapshot of a survivor who understands that she will outlive any heartache of this earth. She rejoices in how God has shaped her through adversity. And now she testifies that God has been with her through the horrible ordeal, and He remains a faithful Friend.

May Stephanie's story and Peter's letter encourage us to live with that same perspective, spirit of resilience, and living hope. Take courage, for by God's grace you will survive!

1. Flint Stories, http://www.flintstories.com/real_funny_stories/realstories.php (accessed February 25, 2010).

2. Doug Murren and Barb Shurin, *Is it Real When it Doesn't Work?* (Nashville, Tenn.: Thomas Nelson Publishers, 1990), 12.

3. William Barclay, *The Letters of James and Peter,* The Daily Study Bible Series (Philadelphia: The Westminster Press, 1976), 167.

4. C. John Weborg, "Covenant Companion," *Christianity Today,* vol. 30, no. 14, July 1986.

5. Jean-Pierre Martinez, "God Is Able," Sermon Central, http://www.sermoncentral.com/sermon.asp?SermonID=50239&ContributorID=8416 (accessed February 25, 2010).

6. Adapted from http://www.epiphanylc.org/sermon071501.html.

7. Adapted from "Twins in Womb Debate Life After Birth," Preaching Today, http://preachingtoday.com/illustrations/article_print.html?id=25292.

8. Kyle Nagel, "Spring Valley Academy Reopens 11 Months After Fire," *Dayton Daily News,* http://www.daytondailynews.com/news/dayton-news/spring-valley-academy-reopens-11spring-valley-academy-reopens-11-months-after-fire--261610.html?cxtype=rss_local-news (accessed February 25, 2010).

9. Brittany Murphy, quoted in *Seventeen Magazine,* September 2003, The Quotations Page, http://www.quotationspage.com/quote/31701.html (accessed February 25, 2010).

10. Michael Hall, "Running for His Life," *Reader's Digest,* March 2004, 112–118.

11. Adapted from Stephanie Fast, "Outcast," Power to Change, http://powertochange.com/experience/spiritual-growth/outcast/ (accessed February 25, 2010).

Chapter 2

SELF-CONTROL

---

1 Peter 1:13–25

For many years Paul Harvey, the famed radio broadcaster, never varied from his routine. The alarm clock would ring at 3:30 A.M. in his twenty-two-room home in River Forest, Illinois. He would brush his teeth, shower, shave, get dressed, eat oatmeal, get into the car, and drive downtown. It took a well-orchestrated forty-five minutes. He dressed in a shirt, coat, and tie, as if going to work as the president of a bank—in sharp contrast to the aggressively informal, slovenly manner common to some radio broadcasters. "It is all about discipline," Harvey says. "I could go to work in my pajamas, but long ago I got some advice from the man who was the engineer for my friend Billy Graham's radio show. He said, . . . if you don't [use self-control] in every area, you'll lose your edge."[1]

In contrast, New York Yankees owner, George Steinbrenner, has paid more than a half-million dollars in fines to Major League Baseball for his *lack* of self-control.[2]

It's no surprise that the Bible urges us to develop this important virtue. Three times in this first letter, Peter gives the command, "be self-controlled." When you live a self-controlled life, you reap immeasurable benefits. Peter is giving us a tip on a better way to do life. He's inviting us to participate in the abundant life that Christ offers.

Listen to Peter, "Be self-controlled; set your hope fully on the grace to be given you when Jesus Christ is revealed. As obedient children, do not conform to the evil desires you had when you lived in ignorance" (1 Peter 1:13, 14).

The Greek word *nepho,* translated "self-controlled," literally means "to

24

abstain from intoxicating drink," but it is consistently employed metaphorically in the New Testament to refer to spiritual sobriety and balance. Peter warns new believers not to conform to their old habits of sin, but instead to show restraint. In this way, Peter claims, it's possible to avoid an insipid life of foolishness. So who wouldn't want to experience the adventure of a disciplined, self-controlled life?

Peter continues by giving three simple principles that represent the best way to live. These guidelines mark the "self-controlled" life.

1. LIVE WITH NOTHING TO HIDE.

First, Peter calls us to live with nothing to hide. Notice the verses that follow, "But just as he who called you is holy, so be holy in all you do; for it is written: 'Be holy, because I am holy' " (verses 15, 16).

Peter is quoting Leviticus 19:2, where the Lord not only proclaims that He is holy, but also calls the children of Israel to be holy as He is holy. The Hebrew word used in the Leviticus passage is *gadosh,* which denotes authenticity and purity. Dan Lucarini observes, " 'Be holy' is a command to God's people that is found throughout the Scriptures. Personal holiness is demanded by Christ, the apostles and the entire Old Testament. Holiness means to be set apart *for* God *from* the world. But reality is tough, and the highway to holiness is very narrow as it winds through our culture of sensuality and materialism. Yet Christians are called to walk that straight and narrow road, a walk that requires us to avoid anything that hints of immorality."[3]

The biblical call to holiness is an invitation to sync your private life with your public life. It's a slam against a duplicitous lifestyle.

When you follow Peter's counsel and live with nothing to hide, you cultivate a deep-down, healthy sense of your self-worth. There's no substitute for this feeling that living with integrity inevitably creates.

Robert Schuller, in his book *Self-Love: the Dynamic Force of Success,* offers an example of the correlation of integrity and self-worth. He includes the story of a young man,

> I was bored one night and went to a neighborhood bar. I met this chick and we started drinking. She was lonely. I was bored. I was unmarried. She was divorced. "Let's go to Las Vegas," she suggested. I looked at the hungry invitation in her sultry eyes and immediately put my glass down, paid the bartender, took her arm and headed for the

car. She snuggled warmly and hungrily close to me. We roared through the night with visions of a hot bed in a Vegas motel. For some strange reason that I cannot explain, I was suddenly gripped by the thought that this was a pretty cheap thing for me to do. I found myself mentally torn at the sexual compulsion to "shack up" with this barfly for whom I had no respect whatsoever. At the same time, glancing at the rear-view mirror, I saw my own eyes. They were the eyes of a potentially wonderful person. I was beginning to feel the disgust and self-loathing that I had known on more than one previous occasion after indulging in a depersonalizing sexual escapade. I pulled over to the shoulder of the road and stopped the car. "What are you doing?" she asked.

"I'm getting out," I answered abruptly. "It's your car. Go on to Vegas if you want to. I don't care what you do. I'll thumb a ride back." I slammed the door shut and watched as she angrily spun the wheels in the gravel and roared furiously away. I stood there alone in the night on a lonely stretch of desert road. Suddenly I felt ten feet tall! I never felt so good in my life! I felt like a triumphant general returning victoriously from a proud battle.[4]

Such is the joy of living a self-controlled life of integrity. Do you aspire to experience this joy? Live with nothing to hide.

2. LIVE WITH NOTHING TO PROVE.

Second, Peter tells us to live with nothing to prove. Let's return to the text,

> Since you call on a Father who judges each man's work impartially, live your lives as strangers here in reverent fear. For you know that it was not with perishable things such as silver or gold that you were redeemed from the empty way of life handed down to you from your forefathers, but with the precious blood of Christ, a lamb without blemish or defect. He was chosen before the creation of the world, but was revealed in these last times for your sake. Through him you believe in God, who raised him from the dead and glorified him, and so your faith and hope are in God (verses 17–21).

Peter labels the way of the world as an "empty way of life." It's a sad commentary that so many people get tripped up trying to find fulfillment through the empty way of the world. You can drive a nice car, excel in the workplace, and have a real fat portfolio of gold and silver—all the trappings of "the good life"—but still have a miserable existence.

Tiger Woods comes to mind. Pastor John Ortberg recently commented on Tiger's troubles,

> Has anybody seen the name Tiger Woods in the news [lately]? . . . Well, we're human beings, so we cannot help desiring the good life. It is wired into us, and we wonder who has it. It seems to be attached to attractiveness, money, recognition, status, pleasure. Now, in our day, celebrities get a lot of attention because we have technology to have access to them all the time, but it's always been this way with the human race. Underneath is always this question[,] *Who has the good life? Who has the good stuff?*
>
> Partly, the public is fascinated by people who have all these assets because we think they must be the ones who are living the good life. And then, if there is a mess, we're fascinated by that because . . . the tone of many, many of the stories in the media is if *we* had all that this celebrity has, we wouldn't mess it up. We'd be smart enough to enjoy the good life. But we think it's connected to all the stuff we think they have.
>
> Now, illusions around this question[,] *what is the good life?* lead to chronic envy, or work-a-holism, or discontent. Eventual pain.[5]

Don't get snookered into thinking that celebrity equals the good life. Peter reminds us that it is "an empty way of life." The Bible says your value is not based on your money or fame or handicap at the country club; rather, your value is based on the blood of Christ. Your worth comes from what Jesus paid to redeem you.

Now when you think about it, this is a very logical argument that Peter makes. After all, how do we determine the value of anything?

For example, Dan Baber posted an item on eBay. With a desire to honor his mother, he posted an auction titled, "Best Mother in the World." The winning bidder would receive an e-mail from his mom, Sue Hamilton, that Baber promised would "make you feel like you are the most special person on the earth."

What was his mom's e-mail worth? Well, ninety-two people bid, pushing the price from a $1 opening to a closing bid of $610. (By the way, I think my mom would send you a nice e-mail at that price!)

Again, I ask: What was Sue Hamilton's e-mail worth? I'll tell you what it was worth: $610. Why? Because that's what someone was willing to pay for it.

The value of anything is determined by what someone will pay for it. Peter reminds us that our value is based on what God was willing to pay in order to redeem us. You are worth the life of God Himself, the "precious blood of Christ."

The Associated Press wire service carried a story that gives us a snapshot of Christ's sacrifice. Dr. Samuel Weinstein is the chief of pediatric cardiothoracic surgery for the Children's Hospital at Montefiore Medical Center in the Bronx, New York. In 2006, he traveled to El Salvador with Heart Care International to provide life-saving operations for less-fortunate children. On this trip, however, it took more than his surgical skills to save the life of eight-year-old Francisco Calderon Anthony Fernandez.

Dr. Weinstein and his team began operating on Francisco's heart shortly before noon. Twelve hours later, the procedure took a deadly turn. "The surgery had been going well, everything was working great, but he was bleeding a lot, and they didn't have a lot of the medicines we would use to stop the bleeding," Weinstein said. "After a while, they said they couldn't give him blood because they were running out and he had a rare type." In fact, Francisco's blood type was B-negative, which—according to the American Red Cross—is present in only 2 percent of the population.

As it was, the only other person in the room with a blood type of B-negative was Dr. Weinstein. Knowing what he had to do, he stepped down from the operating table. As his colleagues continued their precision work, Dr. Weinstein set aside his scalpel, took off his gloves, and began washing his hands and forearms. Then, in the corner of an unfamiliar operating room, the prestigious doctor from one of the most advanced hospitals in the world sat down to give away his own blood.

When he had given his pint, Dr. Weinstein drank some bottled water and ate a Pop-Tart. Then—twenty minutes after stepping away from the table—he rejoined his colleagues. After watching his own blood begin circulating into the boy's small veins, Dr. Weinstein completed the operation that saved Francisco's heart—and his life.[6]

Similarly, we are alive because of the life-saving sacrifice of the Great Physician's blood. When this truth sinks in, we are then empowered to live the self-controlled life because we don't have to feel insecure about our possessions, our performance, or our position in the marketplace. We're free to live with nothing to prove. After all, our value is based on the blood of Jesus!

3. LIVE WITH NOTHING TO GAIN.

A final invitation of the self-controlled life is to live with nothing to gain. In the next verse Peter writes, "Now that you have purified yourselves by obeying the truth so that you have sincere love for your brothers, love one another deeply, from the heart" (verse 22).

"Love unconditionally," Peter tells us, "from the heart." Live with nothing to gain; recklessly spill out your life in serving others. Admittedly, this requires intentionality and self-control, but it is in living this way that we begin to experience life "on earth, as it is in heaven." This is how we live now in the kingdom of God. Let me repeat myself: It's just a better way to do life.

Stanley Hauerwas writes, "We can risk loving as passionately as God loves. For we know that the love God makes possible is no scarce resource that must be hoarded so that it may be distributed in dribs and drabs—a little here and a little there. Love is not a rare commodity; rather, the more we love with the intense particularity of God's love, the more we discover that we have the capacity to love."[7]

Years ago I read a story in Calvin Miller's book *The Philippian Fragment* that's still locked in my memory. Here's an adapted version of this tale that imagines a woman's scroll study in the first century,

One week Phoebe asked a most unusual question: "Will Jesus come before the great tribulation or after it?"

While the question was simple enough, the answers sparked a controversy that rocked the village. Thirty-two women voted *pre* and thirty-two voted *post*. In this ghastly deadlock Phoebe was undecided. She felt the harsh strain of both groups expecting her to cast the winning vote in their favor. Phoebe felt that more time and study were needed to adequately vote. "I am burdened," she said, "by having the weight of our Lord's second coming fall squarely on my shoulders."

Days later, Phoebe was still anguishing over which way to cast her vote. On the one hand, the destruction of the Jewish state by the hated Romans seemed to suggest that there was still time before the event. On the other hand, the persecution of Christians was at an all-time high. This seemed to suggest the great persecution was already happening. There was simply no easy answer.

"Phoebe is just wishy-washy," some of the women chattered after the study. Others said, "If Phoebe doesn't make up her mind soon, she will destroy the unity of our church." Still other women were heard to say, "Let's have Phoebe over for afternoon tea to see if we might persuade her to see the truth."

Day after day the women poured over charts and discussed the end of the world. They showed one another their latest interpretations of the scholars and brought their parchment charts on the final signs of the times. "Of all commands in the scrolls," they reasoned, "surely not one is as important as 'Be ready when He comes.'"

At last the week was over and the time had come for Phoebe to end the eschatological feud. While the women were anxiously awaiting her arrival at the study, however, Phoebe was spotted on her way to the leprosarium with her best friend, Emma. "Don't you care about the end of the world?" Emma asked.

"A little," Phoebe replied, "but I think we're better off to go help the lepers today."

"But what if the women get the date all set and your charts are unmarked?"

Phoebe seemed not to hear. She was carrying a large basket of bandages for the lepers.

"But, Phoebe," Emma blurted out, "Don't you care? Is our Lord coming back before or after the Tribulation? When He comes back, where do you want to be found—in this state of indecision or at the Second Coming study?"

"I want to be found over there," she said, pointing to a circle of low, thatched huts.

A little boy came running toward them from the compound. His face was badly blighted and part of his hand was gone. Turning to the boy Phoebe asked, "When do you think the Lord is coming back, my child?" A single tear salted his cheek.

Emma handed her a bandage and couldn't remember why she thought the question was so important. The only verse in Scripture that seemed to matter in that moment was Mark 12:29–31. "The most important commandment is this: 'Hear, O Israel! The Lord our God is the one and only Lord. And you must love the Lord your God with all your heart, all your soul, all your mind, and all your strength.' The second is equally important: 'Love your neighbor as yourself.' No other commandment is greater than these" (NLT).

No other command is greater than this: Love.

Love unconditionally. Love selflessly. Love unceasingly. Love with no hidden agenda. Love with nothing to gain.

Peter concludes this passage with this reminder,

For you have been born again, not of perishable seed, but of imperishable, through the living and enduring word of God. For,

"All men are like grass,
    and all their glory is like the flowers of the field;
the grass withers and the flowers fall,
    but the word of the Lord stands forever."

And this is the word that was preached to you (verses 23–25).

This *is* the word that was preached to you. Be self-controlled; enjoy living in God's kingdom today. How? Live with nothing to hide, nothing to prove, and nothing to gain. It is the secret of the kingdom, hidden in plain sight.

1. Rick Kogan, "Good Days for Paul Harvey," *Chicago Tribune Magazine,* August 4, 2002, 10.

2. Jeff Blair, "Steinbrenner Speaks," *The Globe and Mail,* www.theglobeandmail .com, February 20, 2002.

3. Dan Lucarini, *Why I Left the Contemporary Christian Music Movement: Confessions of a Former Worship Leader* (Webster, N.Y.: Evangelical Press, 2002), 98.

4. Robert Schuller, *Self-Love: The Dynamic Force of Success* (New York: Hawthorn Books, 1969), 34, 35.

5. John Ortberg, "Smart People, Part One," Menlo Park Presbyterian Church, December 6, 2009, http://mppc.org/sites/default/files/transcripts/091206_jortberg.pdf (accessed March 1, 2010).

6. "Heart Doc Halts Surgery to Donate Blood" Montefiore Medical Center, http://www.montefiore.org/whoweare/stories/Weinstein/ (accessed March 1, 2010).

7. "Context," *Christianity Today,* vol. 34, no. 8, September 15, 1989.

Chapter 3

SANCTIFICATION

———————

1 Peter 2:1–12

Ed Hallowell, author and a senior lecturer at Harvard Medical School, shares the following story:

> One day I was sitting at a counter at a downtown Greenwich pizza parlor. I was splitting a small pepperoni pizza with my five-year-old son, Christian. As we sat there, I could not help but overhear the conversation among three teenage boys who were sitting in the booth directly behind us. They were dressed in tennis whites and had obviously just returned from a morning at their fancy local tennis club. Two of the boys were discussing the faults and foibles of another boy, who was not in attendance. They criticized his tennis play, his mode of dress, and every aspect of his personality. The boy obviously suffered tremendous social isolation and rejection. They laughed as they regaled each other with stories of his various faults and failures.
>
> At one point, one of the boys turned to the third boy, who had been silent during the discussions, and said, "None of us ever want to play with Mike. He's such a nerd. But whenever the coach asks us to choose a partner for doubles, you always choose to play with Mike. Nobody likes Mike. Nobody will play with Mike. Why do you play with him?"
>
> The third boy responded quietly, "*That's* why I play with him."
>
> I looked over my shoulder at that courageous young man, and then I looked at my own son. My fondest hope at that moment was that my

32

son would develop the strength of character and courage that that boy possessed.[1]

THE ADVENTURE OF SANCTIFICATION

The apostle Peter shares that father's sentiment as he writes a letter to Christians. He expressed his fondest hope: That you and I would develop in character; that you and I would mature into the character of Christ. The theological word for this process is *sanctification.*

Jesus called us into this adventure of sanctification when He said, "Be perfect, therefore, as your heavenly Father is perfect" (Matthew 5:48). C. S. Lewis comments, "The command *Be ye perfect* is not idealistic gas. Nor is it a command to do the impossible. [God] is going to make us into creatures that can obey that command."[2] That's exciting news, but how does this transformation happen?

Let's consult the apostle Peter for an answer. Earlier in 1 Peter 1:15, we read the command of God, "Be holy, because I am holy." Now Peter elaborates on this calling to holiness and gives us a picture of what this looks like, "Therefore, rid yourselves of all malice and all deceit, hypocrisy, envy, and slander of every kind. Like newborn babies, crave pure spiritual milk, so that by it you may grow up in your salvation, now that you have tasted that the Lord is good" (2:1–3).

Peter says, "Now that you know that the Lord is good; now that you understand that living according to the principles of the kingdom of heaven is a better way to do life, now that you know, live like it. You begin as a baby, but now it's time to grow up in your salvation."

I've had a few "growing up" moments in my spiritual walk. What about you?

I'm remembering a road trip of nine hours with two kids. Such a trip is like crossing the country on a pogo stick. It's possible, but very difficult.

To help beat five hundred miles of boredom, we armed our kids with a DVD player and a stack of old sitcoms. Over and over we watched the black and white classics of *The Andy Griffith Show.* Remembering the episodes from my childhood, I wanted to expose my children to the hilarious antics of Deputy Sheriff Barney Fife, the cocky but incompetent cop dealing with inconsequential crimes in the hick town of Mayberry, North Carolina.

The episode that hogged the most play time on our trip tells of a spoiled brat moving into town. The kid learned to always get his way by throwing tantrums. That's when he runs into Barney Fife—literally "runs" into him. The boy is racing his bike on the sidewalk and nearly takes out the assistant cop.

Deputy Fife tears into the kid, "Hey, you're not allowed to ride a bike on the sidewalk. . . . Bike riding on the street only, city statute 249A, section roman numeral five."

No sooner does the kid promise to obey than he turns the corner on the sidewalk and plows into the wise and soft-spoken sheriff Andy Taylor. Barney races to the crime scene. "I warned him, and he deliberately rode on the sidewalk again."

"Is that true, son?" Andy asks. "Did you hear Officer Fife warn you?"

"Yes, sir," the kid responds defiantly.

"What you do it again for?"

"Because I wanted to!"

Andy then pieces together an unsolved mystery in Mayberry and points at the boy, "You're the one who's been riding around on the sidewalk knocking people over, ain't you?"

"I'll tell my dad about this! Then you'll be sorry," the kid screams.

Barney whines, "Oooooh go ahead and tell him and see if we care."

The kid sticks out his tongue and scowls in Barney's face, *"Mwhaaaahaa!"*

In an unguarded moment of immaturity, Barney mirrors the kid's contorted face and echoes, *"Mwhaaaahaa!"*

"Ah, Barn," Andy intervenes in his smooth Southern accent, "let's try to keep this on an adult level."

That quickly became the phrase of our trip. Dozens of times my kids parroted, "Ah, let's try to keep this on an adult level."

The context never mattered. I'd say to my five-year-old, "Please pass the ketchup."

"Ah Daaaaaaaad," she'd say with a hint of Kentucky accent, "let's try to keep this on an adult level."

Two hours from home we were road weary and worn out. My wife, Cherié, was driving when she missed the exit, tacking on an extra twenty minutes to the trip.

"How could you miss that exit?" I uncorked. "We've only been on this road a million times. Is nine hours not long enough? Do you need to make it a ten-hour trip?"

My kids were quick to rebuke me. "Ah, Dad," they said in unison, "let's try to keep this on an adult level."

In that case the line fit perfectly. All I could do was to laugh at my immaturity. They were right. I slipped.

Perhaps you can learn from my goof. Next time you're tempted to return gossip with gossip or you want to shame the guy who stole your girlfriend or lash out against the teacher who treated you unfairly, whisper to yourself, "Ah, let's try to keep this on an adult level."

This is the appeal from the apostle Peter, "Ah, Christians, let's try to live on an adult level." He says, "Grow up in your salvation."

THE "HOW?" OF SANCTIFICATION

The question becomes, "How?" Peter answers in the next verses by telling us that we must come to Jesus, the living Stone. He says, "As you come to him, the living Stone—rejected by men but chosen by God and precious to him—you also, like living stones, are being built into a spiritual house to be a holy priesthood, offering spiritual sacrifices acceptable to God through Jesus Christ" (2:4, 5).

Peter says the process of sanctification begins with coming to Jesus. As you live in His presence, He matures you into a holy priesthood. In other words, as you come to the living Stone—who is Christ—you become a living stone; that is, you become like Christ.

You mature as a Christian the same way that a pumpkin becomes a jack-o-lantern. This kind of transformation never happens by the pumpkin working hard to change itself. No, it only happens when an outside power comes and redeems that pumpkin. The miracle of sanctification occurs when God picks you from the patch, brings you in, and washes all the dirt off of you. Then He cuts off the top and scoops out all the yucky stuff inside. He removes the orange seaweed (or whatever it is) and all that nasty goop. Then he carves you a new, smiling face and puts his light inside of you to shine for the world to see.

Next time you see a jack-o-lantern, think about sanctification. When you live in the presence of Jesus, He acts in your behalf. He cleans you up. He resides in you. And you glow with His light.

Next, Peter elaborates on this idea of Christ being the living Stone.

> For in Scripture it says:
> "See, I lay a stone in Zion,
>   a chosen and precious cornerstone,
> and the one who trusts in him
>   will never be put to shame."
> Now to you who believe, this stone is precious. But to those who do not believe,

"The stone the builders rejected
has become the capstone,"

and,

"A stone that causes men to stumble
and a rock that makes them fall."

They stumble because they disobey the message—which is also what they were destined for (verses 6–8).

You can imagine what Peter was thinking when he wrote these words. He speaks of Christ as the Rock. Remember, it was Jesus who gave Peter his nickname "The Rock."

Perhaps Peter was rehearsing the story Jesus told of the wise man and the foolish man. The wise man builds on the rock, and the foolish man on the sand. Peter is parroting this story when he says if you build your life on the Cornerstone, Jesus Christ, you will live—that's wise. But if you build on anything else, you're destined for disappointment and ultimately, death—that's foolish.

In his book *Hearing God's Voice,* Henry Blackaby tells about the first funeral he ever conducted. It was for a three-year-old child. While visiting the family, Blackaby noticed that the girl was quite spoiled. She ignored her parents' instructions. When they told her to come, she'd go the other way. When they said, "sit down," she stood up. Her parents laughed, finding her behavior cute.

One day their front gate was inadvertently left open. The parents saw their child escaping out of the yard and heading toward the road. To their horror, a car was racing down the street. As she ran out between two parked cars, they both screamed at her to stop. She paused for a second, looked back at her parents, then gleefully laughed as she turned and ran directly into the path of the oncoming car.

Blackaby writes, "As a young pastor, this was a profound lesson for me. I realized I must teach God's people not only to recognize His voice but also immediately to obey His voice when they hear it. It is life [or death]."[3]

This is a decision we all face. It is life or death. What are you going to build your life upon? The rock or sand?

Study the story of the wise and foolish builders in Matthew 7:24–27. The obvious question is this: "Why would anyone choose death?" It's pure foolishness.

Throughout the centuries, when children do something foolish, parents ask the same question of their kids—Why? "Why did you stick a bean in your brother's ear?" "Why did you disobey?" "Why did you leave your bike behind the car?" And every child throughout history answers in the same way, "I dunno."

If you were to ask this foolish man, "Why in the world would you build your one and only life on the sand?" What do you think he'd say? "I dunno."

No one plans to build a life on a value system of sand. No one gets involved in a relationship, planning to end up in divorce court. No one experiments with pot, intending to be a homeless addict. No one tries to be estranged from their children by working too much. So why would anyone choose to live like that? "I dunno."

THE CHOICE FOR SANCTIFICATION

You must decide for yourself. You will not drift into sanctification. You will not accidentally build your life on the values of the kingdom of God. This process begins with a choice that says, "I will build my life on the Cornerstone—Jesus Christ. I will connect with God through prayer, worship, and Bible study. Then, as best as I can, I will do whatever God calls me to do. I choose to allow Him to change me from the inside out."

Elbert Hubbard claims, "If your religion does not change you, then you should change your religion."[4] Indeed, authentic spirituality inevitably produces transformation. If you're a Christian but you're not becoming more like Jesus each day, then your religion is worth no more than a stack of Enron stock.

A story flying around the Internet tells of a man being tailgated by a stressed-out woman. He comes to an intersection just as the light turns yellow. He stops. This infuriates the woman behind him. She camps on her horn and punctuates the shrill noise with a few ungodly gestures. Suddenly she hears a policeman tapping on her window. He orders her out of the car and handcuffs her. Then he takes her to the station where she is fingerprinted, photographed, and locked up in a cell.

A couple of hours later, the arresting officer returns and sheepishly explains. "I'm very sorry for the mistake," he begins. "Here's what happened. I pulled up behind your car while you were blowing the horn and cursing and using vulgar gestures. Then I noticed the 'What Would Jesus Do?' bumper sticker on your car and the 'Choose Life' license plate holder and the 'Follow Me to Sunday School' window sign and the Christian fish emblem on your trunk. Naturally, I assumed you had stolen the car."

Friends, the world is weary of people who have Christian bumper stickers on their cars, Christian fish signs on their trunks, Christian books on their shelves, Christian stations preset on their radios, Christian jewelry around their necks, Christian movies in their Blu-ray players, and Christian magazines for their coffee tables, but do not have the love and joy of Christ in their hearts.

CHOSEN FOR SANCTIFICATION

The apostle Peter reminds Christians that we are called to be different from the world. Scripture records, "You are a chosen people, a royal priesthood, a holy nation, a people belonging to God, that you may declare the praises of him who called you out of darkness into his wonderful light. Once you were not a people, but now you are the people of God; once you had not received mercy, but now you have received mercy" (1 Peter 2:9, 10).

Earlier we noted that Peter invites us to experience the adventure of sanctification—that theological concept describing the process of growing into the character of Christ. For this, we are chosen.

One time I was preparing to pour a patio in our backyard. While standing in the middle of seventeen tons of crushed rock, my five-year-old daughter Claire picked up a rock and exclaimed, "Wow! Look, Dad! I found a rock! It's my special rock!"

I examined the rock—which looked identical to the rest of the seventeen tons we were standing in. "And what makes this rock special?" I asked.

"Well, look at it," Claire exclaimed. "It's shaped like a tractor. And it looks kind of sparkly. And it's bigger than a lot of the other rocks."

I examined the rock. I strained to see its uniqueness. But it still looked like every other rock in the pile. Finally I said, "Keep it, Claire. It's a special rock because you chose it."

You, too, are special because God has chosen you. Nobody has your smile or your personality or your exact interests. Peter says, "God has chosen you to be a royal priesthood, a holy nation, a people belonging to God. He has chosen you to be light in this dark world. He has chosen you to receive mercy."

Remember: You are chosen. You are sanctified and growing into the character of Christ. You are chosen to be light in this dark world.

Malcolm Muggeridge writes,

"I am the light of the world," the founder of the Christian religion said. What a stupendous phrase! And how particularly marvelous to-day, when one is conscious of so much darkness in the world! "Let your light shine before men," he exhorted us. You know, sometimes . . . someone asks me what I most want, what I should most like to do in the little that remains of my life, and I always nowadays truthfully answer—and it is truthful—"I should like my light to shine, even if only very fitfully, like a match struck in a dark, cavernous night and then flickering out."[5]

LIVING THE SANCTIFIED LIFE

Peter tells us that we are chosen to let our lights shine, like a match in a dark, cavernous night. Listen again to the apostle, "Dear friends, I urge you, as aliens and strangers in the world, to abstain from sinful desires, which war against your soul. Live such good lives among the pagans that, though they accuse you of doing wrong, they may see your good deeds and glorify God on the day he visits us" (1 Peter 2:11, 12).

It sounds like Jesus talking, doesn't it? Remember the line from the Sermon on the Mount, "Let your light shine before men, that they may see your good deeds and praise your Father in heaven" (Matthew 5:16)?

Peter exhorts us, "You are a chosen people. You are sanctified. Now live like it."

Recently an enthusiastic fan found himself in an elevator with Lee Iacocca, the retired chairman of Chrysler corporation.

"Mr. Iacocca," the man bubbled, "I love your television commercials advertising Chrysler. My favorite is the one with you and your granddaughter. And that one with you and rapper Snoop Dogg, is great."

Iacocca replied, "Sir, I could care less of what you think of my commercials. What I want to know is what kind of car do you drive? Do you drive a Chrysler?"

That's the bottom line. You can advertise that you're a Christian; you can talk in a real churchy voice. You can eat only tofu and tree bark. You can sport the latest WWJD bracelet. But the real question is this: Is Christ being formed in you? Is He driving every decision you make? Peter wonders: Do the pagans see Christ in you such that they glorify God in heaven? If this process of sanctification is not happening in a Christian's life, then the person is not an authentic follower of Christ.

Myron Augsburger writes, "The words *holiness* and *sanctification* are not prominent in much of Protestant theology. We have tended to speak of justification without a commensurate emphasis on sanctification. . . . Holiness means that one belongs wholly to God. This is also the meaning of sanctification, being set apart as God's own possession."[6]

Peter goes on to say that when this transformation takes place, pagans will notice Christians and, consequently, glorify God. As Sheldon Vanauken puts it, "The best argument for Christianity is Christians: their joy, their certainty, their completeness. But the strongest argument against Christianity is also Christians—when they are somber and joyless, when they are self-righteous and smug in complacent consecration, when they are narrow and repressive, then Christianity dies a thousand deaths."[7]

So may I meddle for a moment? What kind of a witness are you for Christ? When pagans see you, do they naturally want to glorify God? Are you being sanctified? That is, are you becoming more and more like Jesus each day? Are you being transformed into a new creation?

Allow me to give you a picture of what that looks like in real life. Stephen Baldwin is one of the famous Baldwin brothers from the family of Hollywood actors.

Stephen changed when he met Christ. Listen to his testimony, "I've never been as excited or happy about where I am in my life. There's no one I know in Hollywood who can say that."

Stephen's wife accepted Christ in 2000 and said, "I'm going to be serving Jesus now." Confused by her conversion, Stephen thought, *Who does this Jesus think he is, coming around here?*

But the events of September 11 changed Stephen's mind. He realized that the impossible was possible. Stephen says, "It made me say the Bible is true, and Jesus Christ could come back tomorrow."

How has his life changed? Stephen's work as an actor "has largely dried up." He won't work in a film that includes adultery, violence, or profanity.

He traded his Porsche for a Chevy Malibu.

Stephen spends his available time preaching the gospel. He directs and hosts a DVD project aimed at reaching young people through extreme sports.

As for his marriage, Stephen and his wife are now "as one." Stephen truly is a new creation.[8]

That is God's dream for you. He longs to make you into a new creation.

"What this means," Paul tells us in 2 Corinthians 5:17, "is that those who become Christians become new persons. They are not the same anymore, for the old life is gone. A new life has begun!" (NLT).

"A new life"—sounds inviting, doesn't it? The good news is that this miracle of sanctification can happen to you. How? Well, it only happens if you are "in Christ." Sanctification never happens by trying real hard to be good. It's not by trying hard to be like Jesus that we are transformed; rather, it happens by training. As we engage in training through the spiritual disciplines of prayer, Bible study, serving the poor, corporate worship, etc., we are catapulted into the presence of Christ. It is there in the presence of He who is holy that we become holy.

Think about it this way: If you hear that someone is "into golf," what does that mean? It probably means that this person subscribes to *Golf Digest,* she studies "how-to" books on golf, she practices putting, she heads to the golf course every weekend. In other words, she arranges her life around the priority of maturing as a golfer.

So when Paul calls us to be "in Christ," what exactly does he mean? He is telling us to arrange our lives around the priority of maturing as Christians. That could involve subscribing to a good Christian magazine, studying God's manual, practicing Christlike acts of compassion, and heading to church every week.

In the end, that's how sanctification happens. As we live *in Christ,* we become *like Christ.*

1. Edward M. Hallowell, *Connect: Twelve Vital Ties That Open Your Heart, Lengthen Your Life, and Deepen Your Soul* (New York: Pantheon Books, 1999), 258, 259.

2. C. S. Lewis, *Mere Christianity* (n.p.: C. S. Lewis Pte Ltd., 1980), quoted in "Reflections," *Christianity Today,* August 21, 2000.

3. Henry Blackaby, *Hearing God's Voice* (Nashville, Tenn.: Broadman & Holman, 2002), quoted in *Men of Integrity,* May/June 2003.

4. Elbert Hubbard, quoted in "Daily Inspirations," February 25, 2010, http://hopenewscanada.blospot.com/2010_02_01_archive.html.

5. Malcolm Muggeridge, *Jesus Rediscovered,* (Garden City, N.Y.: Doubleday & Company, Inc., 1969), 52.

6. Myron S. Augsburger, *The Christ-Shaped Conscience,* quoted in *Christianity Today,* vol. 37, no. 3.

7. Sheldon Vanauken, *A Severe Mercy* (New York: Harper & Row, 1987), 85.

8. "Baldwin's Great Awakening," *The Week,* November 5, 2004, 12.

Chapter 4

SUBMISSION TO THE GOVERNMENT

---

1 Peter 2:13–17

Paula Zahn of CNN once interviewed Bob Meyers, the brother of Dean Meyers, who was slain on October 9, 2002, by sniper John Muhammad in Manassas, Virginia. Zahn wondered if Meyers was bitter toward the government for not adequately protecting his brother. Meyer's replied, "No, I would say that there isn't a bitterness. I believe that those responsible have to deal with the authorities that God has instituted. First, He instituted human government—and also God says that He'll avenge losses. So we defer to those two authorities and obey the Scripture that indicates that we're not to avenge ourselves as individuals."[1]

It's hard for me to imagine how difficult it must be to lose a brother; but then to harbor no bitterness toward civic leaders for allowing such an unnecessary and tragic death is even more remarkable. I admire Bob Meyers for his mature attitude of submission toward authority.

This attitude of submission is what Peter calls us to model. In his letter to persecuted Christians, Peter devotes a lengthy portion to the topic of submission. First, he talks about submitting to governmental authority, then he calls for submission in the workplace, and finally he addresses submission in a marriage.

First, notice 1 Peter 2:13, 14, where Christians are given this counsel, "Submit yourselves for the Lord's sake to every authority instituted among men: whether to the king, as the supreme authority, or to governors, who are sent by him to punish those who do wrong and to commend those who do right."

Notice that Peter calls us to submit to state authorities. Remember that the recipients of Peter's letter in the first century are being tortured under the cruel reign of Nero, the emperor of Rome. Nevertheless, Peter makes it clear that Christians are to obey civil authorities. Of course this does not mean that we are to violate God's laws in order to obey the dictates of man. Peter himself, when standing on trial before the Sanhedrin, said, "We ought to obey God rather than men" (Acts 5:29, NKJV). Our allegiance is first to Jesus Christ. Ultimately, He is in charge of our lives.

A frustrated mom was struggling with her strong-willed, three-year-old son, Thomas. She looked him in the eye and asked a question sure to knock him into line: "Thomas, who is in charge here?" Not missing a beat, her Sabbath-School-born-and-bred toddler replied, "Jesus is." How can a Christian parent argue with that?

While acknowledging that Christ is ultimately in charge, the general principle stands: Christians must be good and useful citizens of the countries where they live.

Peter's instruction on this topic is consistent with the rest of the New Testament. Jesus said, "Give to Caesar what is Caesar's, and to God what is God's" (Matthew 22:21). In Romans 13, Paul taught that those who govern the nation are sent by God and should be respected. In 1 Timothy 2:2, we're told to pray for kings and leaders in authority.

Peter goes on to explain why it is so important to submit to state authorities. "It is God's will that by doing good you should silence the ignorant talk of foolish men" (1 Peter 2:15). By leading lives of holiness and integrity, we quiet the critics who would accuse us of wrong-doing. Let's face it: everyone is impressed with godly behavior.

I am reminded of the man who went to a fast-food chicken place and bought a nine-piece bucket of chicken. He went to the park for a romantic picnic with his lady.

Upon digging into the bucket, however, he got a big surprise. Instead of chicken, he discovered the restaurant's night deposit—nine thousand dollars! The young man returned to the restaurant and asked for his chicken in exchange for the money. The manager, in awe of the young man's honesty, asked for his name and told him he wanted to call the newspaper and the local news station to do a story on him. He would be a local hero, an example of honesty that would inspire others.

This is what Peter is talking about: by doing good, others are impressed. They take notice, just as the manager did in the case of this honest chicken-eater.

But now for the rest of the story: The hungry man shrugged it off. He said, "My date's waiting. I just want my order of chicken."

The manager was now even more impressed. "You're not only a man of integrity," he said, "but you're also a person of deep humility. This makes your story even more compelling. Please, I must share your story with the local media."

By now the hungry man was visibly agitated. He shouted, "Just get my chicken, would you?"

"I don't get it," the manager replied. "You're an honest man in a dishonest world. This is the perfect opportunity to inspire others toward integrity. Please, give me your name and also the woman's name. Is that your wife?"

"That's my problem," the young man confessed. "My wife is at home. The woman in the car is my girlfriend. Now let me have my chicken so I can get out of here."

When Peter challenges us to do good, he's not talking about just looking good on the outside. This is not about some charade of devotion. No, Peter's appeal throughout this letter is to "be holy." New Testament scholar Paul Cedar, explains, "Peter returns to one of the basic themes of this epistle—that of holy conduct. He reminds us vividly that God is not merely concerned with our profession; He is concerned with our possession—our lifestyle. He desires that we live holy and honorable lives; that our 'conduct' may be observed as good by outsiders."[2]

Peter then writes in verses 16 and 17, "Live as free men, but do not use your freedom as a cover-up for evil; live as servants of God. Show proper respect to everyone: Love the brotherhood of believers, fear God, honor the king."

Here you find a succinct strategy for submission. It's too easy to read through Peter's letter and theoretically agree that it's a good idea to practice submission toward state authorities. But Peter won't let us get away with just agreeing in some hypothetical sort of way. He gets practical now and tells us what submission looks like in real life. He offers three challenges for those of us who would take seriously this summons to submission.

1. LOVE THE BROTHERHOOD.

First, we must "love the brotherhood of believers." A simple and practical way to carry out the calling to submission is to love the "brotherhood of believers," that is, the church. Joshua Harris, in his book *Stop Dating the Church,* adds this perspective,

The strongest argument I know for why you and I should love and care about the Church is that Jesus does. The greatest motivation we could ever find for being passionately committed to the Church is that Jesus is passionately committed to the Church. . . .

Christians often speak of wanting God's heart for the poor or the lost. And these are good desires. But shouldn't we also want God's heart for the Church? If Jesus loves the Church, you and I should, too. It's that simple.[3]

Peter gives us the same challenge when he calls us to love the church.

2. FEAR GOD.

The second command from Peter is to "fear God." You see, submission includes a humble recognition of God's sovereignty.

In his book *The Three Christs of Ypsilanti,* psychologist Milton Rokeach describes three of his patients at a psychiatric hospital in Ypsilanti, Michigan. These men, Leon, Joseph, and Clyde, refused to fear God or practice submission. Instead each one suffered from "psychotic delusional grandiose disorder." Put simply, each one thought of himself as God. For two years Rokeach labored with them, but healing seemed hopeless.

In desperation Rokeach put them in close proximity with one another, thinking this might cause them to see beyond their own grandiose delusions. This led to some interesting discussions. One of the men would claim, "I am the Messiah. I am on a mission to save the earth."

"How do you know?" Rokeach would ask.

"God told me."

Another patient would counter, "I never told you such a thing!"

It's hard to know whether to laugh or cry at their story. But do you suppose we all suffer from a messiah complex? It may not be severe enough to land in Ypsilanti, but it's just as irrational as Leon, Joseph, and Clyde's condition. This delusion is as old as the Garden of Eden, when the serpent tempted Eve by saying, "You will be like God" (Genesis 3:5).

I have heard it said, "The biggest difference between you and God is that God never thinks He's you." Whenever you fear God by admitting that only God is God, and then trusting Him fully as God, you practice the spiritual art of submission.

3. HONOR THE KING.

Returning now to 1 Peter, we're told there are three ways to practice submission, "Love the brotherhood of believers, fear God," and finally, "honor the king." In other words, live as an exemplary citizen. Respect authority. Obey the laws of the land.

Justin Martyr once wrote to the king, "Everywhere, we, more readily than all men, endeavour to pay to those appointed by you the taxes, both ordinary and extraordinary, as we have been taught by Jesus. We worship only God, but in other things we will gladly serve you, acknowledging you as kings and rulers of men, and praying that, with your kingly power, you may be found to possess also sound judgment."[4]

Another helpful and honest perspective in finding this balance between serving heavenly and earthly authorities comes in the prayer of Donald L. Roberts, president and CEO of Goodwill Industries Manasota. He offered this prayer at the spring 2000 opening of the Florida Senate.

Holy and Eternal God, it must be great to be God, to get what you want—when you want it—how you want it. We mere mortals are not that lucky. We are always having to compromise to get what we want. We call the process "politics." You see, O Lord, we find Senator Jennings' priority number one is Senator McKay's priority number five and Governor Bush's priority number ten; and Senator Carlton doesn't even know it's on the agenda while Secretary of State Kathryn Harris is busy closing down shop. In the midst of all this "politicking" during Session, we know we are supposed to "Be still and know" your will for our lives and all the people of the State of Florida—with every lobbyist in the world bugging us to death. So, God, while we acknowledge you never said discipleship would be easy, we do call upon you to come and be in these Senate Chambers today. Thank you, Lord, the Session is almost over, the budget deal is cut, education got some more money, we cut a few taxes, and in the end, most everyone in this chamber didn't get everything they wanted. And that's the good news. That's politics, Lord, and unless you want to move over and give us the job of being God, which some of us think is our birthright, we will have to muddle along being satisfied with being the best politicians you can create. It's the fun part of being human. In the name of the God of all things, even politics and politicians and in rare instances a lobbyist or two, Amen.[5]

I, too, pray that God would help you to find balance in that delicate dance of submitting to God and government. May the words of this verse be played out in your life. As *The Message* translation puts it, "Love your spiritual family. Revere God. Respect the government."

1. "Victim's Brother Reacts to Sniper Case Arrests," CNN.com, October 24, 2002, http://archives.cnn.com/2002/US/South/10/24/cnna.bob.meyers/index.html (accessed March 4, 2010).

2. Paul A. Cedar, *The Communicator's Commentary: James, 1, 2 Peter, Jude,* ed. Lloyd J. Ogilvie (Waco, Tex.: Word Publishing Group, 1984), 145.

3. Joshua Harris, *Stop Dating the Church* (Sisters, Ore.: Multnomah Publishers, 2004), 31.

4. Justin Martyr, *Apology* 1:17, quoted in William Barclay, *The Letter to the Romans,* The Daily Study Bible Series (Philadelphia, Pa.: The Westminster Press, 1975), 172.

5. Ted Olsen, "A Surprising Opening Prayer," The Way We Believe Now, According to The New York Times Blog, posted May 8, 2000, ChristianityToday.com, http://www.christianitytoday.com/ct/2000/mayweb-only/12.0a.html?start=1 (accessed March 4, 2010).

Chapter 5

SUBMISSION TO THE BOSS

---

1 Peter 2:18–25

Author and educator Howard Hendricks tells of sitting in a plane that was delayed for takeoff. After a long wait, the passengers became more and more cranky. Hendricks noticed how graciously one of the flight attendants interacted with the ornery passengers. After takeoff, he commented to the flight attendant how impressed he was with her poise and self-control. He explained that he wanted to write a letter of commendation for her to the airline. The stewardess replied, "I don't work for the airline company; I work for Jesus Christ."

Working for Christ adds a new dimension to the idea of submission, doesn't it? Driven by your devotion, you are not just submitting to your employer, but to Jesus.

After addressing what submission to governmental authority is all about, Peter broadens this idea of submission to include the workplace. He reminds us that we don't work for Pfizer or Microsoft or Walmart; no, we work for Jesus Christ.

Listen to the apostle, "Slaves, submit yourselves to your masters with all respect, not only to those who are good and considerate, but also to those who are harsh" (1 Peter 2:18). Peter specifically addresses the working class of his day. Keep in mind that there were sixty million slaves in the Roman Empire. William Barclay points out that slaves were not limited to performing menial tasks but worked as doctors, teachers, actors, secretaries, musicians, and a wide range of other professions. It was not the case that slaves in the ancient world were always abused and unhappy. Many slaves were valued and trusted members of the family. But in all cases, slaves possessed no rights. Every slave was considered to be the property of the master.

Aristotle once wrote, "There can be no friendship nor justice towards inanimate things; indeed, not even towards a horse or an ox, nor yet towards a slave as a slave. For master and slave have nothing in common; a slave is a living tool, just as a tool is an inanimate slave."[1]

So in this passage Peter is calling the working class to labor with a spirit of submission. He continues, "For it is commendable if a man bears up under the pain of unjust suffering because he is conscious of God. But how is it to your credit if you receive a beating for doing wrong and endure it? But if you suffer for doing good and you endure it, this is commendable before God" (verses 19, 20).

Peter clarifies that if the employee suffers pain by his or her own doing, that's one thing. But if that worker endures mistreatment for "doing good," then that is commendable before God. The word *commendable* literally translates to mean "worthy of divine favor." *The Seventh-day Adventist Bible Commentary* explains this verse by saying, "The Christian [worker] should never be guilty of laziness, inefficiency, or dishonesty, for which pagan [workers] were often punished. God has ways of compensating the faithful believers who suffer for righteousness' sake, and this warm assurance of His concern sustains their faith and courage."[2]

"To this you were called," Peter goes on to say in the next verse, "because Christ suffered for you, leaving you an example, that you should follow in his steps" (verse 21).

If you care to know how to conduct yourself in the workplace, look at Jesus. Follow "in His steps."

That was Truett Cathy's intent when he opened his first restaurant in 1946. From that humble beginning his business has grown to over 1,300 Chick-fil-A restaurants across the United States with more than $1.5 billion in annual sales. Cathy's desire to do business in the steps of Jesus is clear in Chick-fil-A's purpose statement, "That we might glorify God by being a faithful steward in all that is entrusted to our care, and that we might have a positive influence on all the people that we might come in contact with."

So what does that look like in practical terms? From the beginning the company has followed a policy of closing all restaurants on Sunday. No doubt this practice has cost Cathy millions of dollars in business; he insists that it gives employees a day to spend with God and family. Moreover, Chick-fil-A sponsors a boys and girls camp through a foundation founded more than twenty years ago by Cathy. The WinShape Centre Foundation has also sponsored and built fourteen foster homes. The WinShape Family Centre also offers marital conferences and retreats for entire families. Chick-fil-A has placed a Bible in every school throughout the entire state of Georgia. These are a few of the practical ways that Cathy attempts to do business "in His steps." (By the way, I'm not sponsored by Chick-fil-A, but I am impressed with anyone who seeks to do business in the steps of Jesus.)

THE JESUS WAY

After calling us to follow in His steps, Peter describes Jesus in this way,

> " 'He committed no sin, and no deceit was found in his mouth.' When they hurled their insults at him, he did not retaliate; when he suffered, he made no threats. Instead, he entrusted himself to him who judges justly. He himself bore our sins in his body on the tree, so that we might die to sins and live for righteousness; by his wounds you have been healed. For you were like sheep going astray, but now you have returned to the Shepherd and Overseer of your souls" (verses 22–25).

Peter explains that Jesus did not retaliate. He forgave and sealed this reconciliation with His own blood on the tree at Calvary. By His wounds we are healed. Now we are called to forgive in the same manner as Christ forgave.

Just think about the radical nature of this calling. Remember, Peter is talking here to slaves; he is calling them to respond to insults and mistreatment with the love of Jesus.

Out of the ashes of apartheid, we find an extraordinary example of this principle. Apartheid was the official policy of racial segregation in South Africa. In plain terms, apartheid was the practice of slavery. I lived in South Africa for a year when apartheid was in full force, and it meant "Whites Only" signs on certain beaches, separate bathrooms for whites, coloreds, and blacks, and open sewage streaming through the streets of black townships like Soweto.

In the past twenty years, we have seen dramatic changes in this evil system. Nelson Mandela was released from prison and elected as president. Archbishop Desmond Tutu headed the government panel called the Truth and Reconciliation Commission.

The rules for the TRC were straightforward: if a white police officer or army official confessed to a crime, admitting guilt, he would not be punished for any wrongdoing. Some complained that it wasn't fair to allow crimes to go unrequited, but Mandela prevailed in his view that healing was more important than justice.

At one hearing, a South African woman listened in a courtroom while white police officers described the crimes they had perpetrated in the name of apartheid. A policeman named van de Broek admitted to the murder of this woman's son. At point-blank range he pulled the trigger on her eighteen-year-old boy. He then partied with his police buddies while they burned his body, rolling it over and over in the fire like a piece of barbeque meat.

Eight years later, van de Broek and others returned to the old woman's home to seize her husband, the boy's father. Shortly after midnight, van de Broek grabbed the woman and forced her to watch as they strapped her husband to a woodpile. They drenched him with gasoline and ignited the flames that consumed his body. The last words she heard her husband say were "Forgive them."

The drama mounted in the courtroom as this woman was given an opportunity to address the man who had murdered her husband and her son. "What do you want to say to him?" the judge asked.

"I want to say three things," she said calmly. "I want Mr. van de Broek to take me to the place where they burned my husband's body. I would like to gather up the dust and give him a decent burial." His head down, the policeman nodded agreement.

"Second, Mr. van de Broek took all my family away from me, and I still have a lot of love to give. Twice a month, I would like for him to come to the ghetto and spend a day with me so I can be a mother to him."

Then she added her final request. "Third, I would like Mr. van de Broek to know that he is forgiven by God, and that I forgive him too. I would like someone to lead me to where he is seated, so I can embrace him and he can know my forgiveness is real."

As the elderly woman was escorted across the courtroom, van de Broek fainted, overwhelmed. Someone began to sing, "Amazing Grace, how sweet the sound. . . ." Soon everyone joined in.

What happened in the courtroom that day truly was amazing. What happened, in a word, was "grace."

Peter challenges you and me to also live as conduits of God's grace. Whether you're a CEO, a student, a nurse, a truck driver, or a stay-at-home parent, you will have an opportunity today to administer God's grace to others. Perhaps that means biting your tongue when a co-worker baits you to malign the boss. Maybe it means doing the dirty jobs without being asked or thanked. Or it could mean pursuing reconciliation with that scoundrel who ripped you off.

Whatever it means in your situation, God calls you to do it. By practicing submission you are living out the calling of the cross and building the kingdom of Christ.

1. Aristotle, quoted in William Barclay, *The Letters of James and Peter*, The Daily Study Bible Series (Philadelphia: The Westminster Press, 1975), 211.

2. Francis Nichol, ed., *The Seventh-day Adventist Bible Commentary*, vol. 7 (Hagerstown, Md.: Review and Herald® Publishing Association, 1980), 566.

Chapter 6

SUBMISSION IN A MARRIAGE

---

1 Peter 3:1–7

The journal *Housekeeping Monthly,* dated May 13, 1955, published an article entitled "The Good Wife's Guide." It includes a list of what wives should do in order to be a "good wife."

Here are some excerpts:

> Have dinner ready. . . . Most men are hungry when they come home and the prospect of a good meal (especially his favorite dish!) is part of the warm welcome needed.
>
> Listen to him. You may have a dozen important things to tell him, but the moment of his arrival is not the time. Let him talk first—remember, his topics of conversation are more important than yours.
>
> Don't complain if he's home late for dinner or even if he stays out all night. Count this as minor compared to what he might have gone through that day.
>
> Remember, he is the master of the house and, as such, will always exercise his will with fairness and truthfulness. You have no right to question him.
>
> A good wife always knows her place.

Can you believe this was published less than sixty years ago? My how the world has changed!

Actually, there are some who interpret our next verse in Peter to say the same thing to wives as the *Housekeeping Monthly* article does. (These interpreters, of course, are all male!)

As we journey through the book of 1 Peter, we come to this passage in which Peter calls on wives to be submissive to their husbands. A cartoon comes to mind that pictures a preacher who had transformed his pulpit area into a fortress. He is peering through the crack of a machine gun nest. The caption reads, "Today my text is 'Wives submit to your husbands.' " Indeed this verse has been quite vexing to wives through the centuries.

But this part of Peter's letter is so much more than a guide for the good wife; the full passage includes guides for the good husband and the good Christian, as well.

A GUIDE FOR THE GOOD WIFE

First, let's consider Peter's guide for the good wife. He writes, "Wives, in the same way be submissive to your husbands" (1 Peter 3:1).

Remember that Peter has called for us to be submissive to governmental authorities; he then appealed for us to practice submission in the workplace; and now, he applies this idea of submission in a God-honoring marriage.

It's important that we understand the original intent of Peter's command here lest we impose on ancient words a twenty-first century meaning the author never intended. When Peter calls for wives to be submissive, he is not commanding them to become doormats to be manipulated by some superior gender. The idea here is not a spineless submission; rather, it is a voluntary selflessness. William Barclay explains, "It is the submission which is based on the death of pride and the desire to serve. It is the submission not of fear but of perfect love."[1] Submission is not a forced deal but rather a willing choice that flows out of a selfless heart.

Let me give you a picture of this. Country singer June Carter Cash, who died in 2003, won awards and achieved world renown, but her love for her husband, Johnny Cash, was most important to her. Her marriage was marked by selfless submission.

Brian Mansfield reported in *USA Today,*

> June likely could have achieved greater career success in any of several entertainment fields: singing, writing, acting. Instead, she picked a supporting role.
>
> "I chose to be Mrs. Johnny Cash in my life," she [said]. . . . "I

decided I'd allow him to be Moses and I'd be Moses' brother Aaron, picking his arms up. . . .

"I stayed in submission to my husband, and he allowed me to do anything I wanted to. I felt like I was lucky to have that kind of romance."[2]

Warren Wiersbie offers this insight,

Submission is not subjugation. Subjugation turns a person into a thing, destroys individuality, and removes all liberty. Submission makes a person become more of what God wants him to be; it brings out individuality; it gives him the freedom to accomplish all that God has for his life and ministry. Subjugation is weakness; it is the refuge of those who are afraid of maturity. Submission is strength; it is the first step toward true maturity and ministry.[3]

So Peter writes,

Wives, in the same way be submissive to your husbands so that, if any of them do not believe the word, they may be won over without words by the behavior of their wives, when they see the purity and reverence of your lives. Your beauty should not come from outward adornment, such as braided hair and the wearing of gold jewelry and fine clothes (1 Peter 3:1–3).

Peter is not talking about the evils of jewelry, braided hair, makeup, or fine clothes. I have been asked, "Is it a sin for women to wear makeup?" Frankly, I think it's a sin for some women to not wear makeup! I agree with Morris Venden when he said, "If the barn needs painting, paint it!" Peter is not indicting women who wear jewelry or makeup, he is talking about how to influence people. It's not by external beauty, but rather internal beauty.
Let's keep reading.

Instead, it should be that of your inner self, the unfading beauty of a gentle and quiet spirit, which is of great worth in God's sight. For this is the way the holy women of the past who put their hope in God used to make themselves beautiful. They were submissive to their own husbands, like Sarah, who obeyed Abraham and called him her master.

You are her daughters if you do what is right and do not give way to fear (verses 4–6).

Now consider what was happening in the ancient world. Many wives of notable Roman citizens became Christians; consequently, they would no longer participate in pagan orgies at the Roman temples. This infuriated the husbands. So Peter addresses this issue by helping women to understand how to influence their husbands toward Christian faith.

It's difficult to appreciate how much courage this took for women in that culture to have the guts to defy the husband and join the Christian church. For a wife to change her religion apart from her husband was unthinkable.

Under Jewish law a woman was an object. The husband owned her like he owned a horse or a house. In the Greek culture, by law the woman was "to remain indoors and to be obedient to her husband." Under Roman law, the woman was under *patria potestas,* the father's power. If and when she married, she was then under the complete authority of her husband.

Peter writes to these women. He's not saying they must dress like unmade beds; he's telling them how to influence their husbands toward Christ. This is not done through external means—braids, jewelry, fine clothes, and so on—but through internal beauty. We influence others through integrity, character, and internal beauty.

The best way to influence someone is through integrity. Let me illustrate.

Fresh out of the seminary, I shopped around for the best deal I could find on a new car. I was trading in a Nissan 200SX that had serious personality disorders. The Auburn dealer said I could drive away in a new Corolla for $2,000 and my trade-in. That sounded good until I went to a Tacoma dealership.

I met a salesman named Mark and explained that I would give him my Nissan along with a thousand bucks. He punched his calculator, scribbled some numbers on scratch paper, and then did something I will never forget. He leaned back in his high-back leather chair, scratched his head, and said, "I think you could get the trade for six hundred dollars less than that."

I was too stunned to speak.

He repeated, "I'd offer four hundred dollars with the car."

"OK! That's my offer."

With that, he escaped to his manager's office. Within two minutes he was back telling me the offer had been accepted.

Well I believe in the cliché that "If it sounds too good to be true, it is." So I said, "Let me think about it."

"No problem. Think about it, and if you want to buy it tomorrow, then just come back. I'll be here."

I returned to the Auburn dealer. He looked at me as if I had the word *fool* tattooed on my forehead. He said, "There is no way a dealer would cut you that kind of a deal. You look like you're more intelligent than that. Don't fall for it."

The next morning I called the Tacoma dealership and talked to Mark again. He assured me his deal was still good. I went down and within fifteen minutes I drove out with a new car. (I recently sold that car with 300,000 miles on it. It ran perfectly, and I never had any problem with it.)

A couple years later I wanted to purchase a pickup. Since we had moved, I went to a dealer in Everett. Once again, I met a salesman by the name of Mark. I played the game until we were within one hundred dollars of making a deal. I was getting ready to walk when another salesman mumbled something behind me. I didn't hear what he had said, so I asked Mark, "What did that guy say?"

Mark was allusive but when I pressed him he said there was another buyer for the pickup if I didn't take it.

I instinctively shot back, "I'll take it for your price." About a half hour later while I was still waiting to speak with the lady in the finance office, I overheard Mark and this other salesman who had walked behind me. They were reveling at their trick in duping me by using one of the oldest tricks in the auto industry. "That sucker actually thought we had another buyer!" they joked.

Now, both salesmen—the one at Tacoma and the one at Everett—sold me a vehicle. Both of the Marks influenced me. But only one earned my respect and would ever score my repeat business. Can you guess which one?

The best way to influence someone is through inner beauty—integrity, character, and a gentle spirit. That is Peter's message to wives.

A GUIDE FOR THE GOOD HUSBAND

Next, Peter offers the good husband's guide. "Husbands, in the same way be considerate as you live with your wives, and treat them with respect as the weaker partner and as heirs with you of the gracious gift of life, so that nothing will hinder your prayers" (verse 7).

Now why is there just one verse addressed to the husbands and six verses to the wives? Is it because men have no issues when it comes to marriage and romance? I'm afraid not.

Remember, Peter is talking about the best way to influence others. In the ancient world, if men converted to Christianity, then the women would follow, and it would not have been an issue as it would have been for women converts. But another reason can be seen in the phrase "in the same way." In other words, everything that Peter just said to the wives, applies to husbands "in the same way." So husbands you, too, are to be submissive—that is, you are to selflessly serve your mate in the same way they are to serve you. This is not a statement of superiority of one gender over another. Peter is an equal opportunity implorer—and he implores husbands to follow the same counsel that he gave to wives.

Peter's plea to husbands is to treat "the weaker partner" with respect because in that culture the husband held power over the wife. The Christian husband will not abuse his power.

Craig Brian Larson illustrates by citing an Associated Press release dated June 6, 2007. At 3:30 p.m., Ben Carpenter., a twenty-one-year-old man with muscular dystrophy, drove his electric-powered wheelchair down the sidewalk in Paw Paw, Michigan. As he approached the street crossing at the corner of Red Arrow Highway at Hazen Street, a semitruck came to a halt at the stoplight. Ben began to cross the street just a few feet in front of the towering truck.

When the light turned green, somehow the fifty-two-year-old driver of the truck did not see Ben in his wheelchair. With Ben still in front of the truck, the engine roared to life, and the mammoth vehicle pulled forward. When the truck struck Ben's wheelchair, the wheelchair turned, now facing forward, and the handles in the back of the wheelchair became wedged in the truck's grille. The wheelchair kept rolling, though, and Ben, wearing a seatbelt, was held in his chair. The truck driver was still oblivious to the fact that he had hit the wheelchair. The truck picked up speed, soon reaching fifty miles per hour. Still the wheelchair and Ben were pinned dangerously on the front.

While the driver continued along in his own little world of the truck cab, people along the road saw what was happening. Everyone but the driver seemed to see the drama unfolding. Frantic observers called 9-1-1. People waved their arms and tried to get the driver's attention. Two off-duty policemen saw what was happening and began to pursue the truck.

On drove the trucker.

On the road behind the truck were two new parallel lines that marked where the wheelchairs' rubber wheels were being worn off. Finally, after two terrifying miles, the driver pulled into a trucking company parking lot, still clueless to the presence of Ben Carpenter pinned to the front of his truck. Thankfully, Ben was unharmed.

Listen, now, as Craig Brian Larson applies the news story to Peter's guide for good husbands,

> The frightening picture of a many-ton truck pushing a small wheel-chair can serve as a metaphor for some relationships we have in life. Just as a truck driver is in a big and powerful position and a person in a wheelchair is in a vulnerable position, so some people have powerful positions in life and others have vulnerable places. To varying degrees, powerful people have control; vulnerable people are controlled by others. For example, . . . husbands have power, as do employers, leaders, pastors, denominational officials, and government officials. By contrast, those who are small or weak are often vulnerable, as are the sick, the poor, the young, the elderly, the debtors, the uneducated.
>
> Power is not wrong; in fact, God gives people power and authority to use for the good of others. When God gives people power, he commands them to use it carefully and responsibly. Many powerful people are careful with their power. Others, tragically, resemble this truck driver flying down the highway with a vulnerable person pinned to the grille of their 18-wheeler.[4]

A GUIDE FOR GOOD CHRISTIANS

Next Peter fleshes out this idea of submission by challenging all who claim the name of Christ to live with an attitude of selfless service. He writes, "Finally, all of you, live in harmony with one another; be sympathetic, love as brothers, be compassionate and humble. Do not repay evil with evil or insult with insult, but with blessing, because to this you were called so that you may inherit a blessing" (verses 8, 9).

Most of us would applaud Peter's counsel to love our enemies—at least theoretically. Unknown enemies on the other side of the world are much easier to love than the irritating neighbor next door.

Last year during the war in Iraq, one American soldier discovered how proximity changes things. Stephen Tschiderer had an opportunity to put Peter's counsel into practice. He's an army medic who met his enemy's bullet before he met his enemy. While patrolling the dangerous streets of Baghdad, Tschiderer was shot in the chest by an enemy sniper. Tschiderer was saved by his bulletproof vest.

A combat team tracked down the sniper; Tschiderer discovered his assailant had been wounded. At this point, loving one's enemy was no longer a theoretical concept. The enemy was directly in front of Tschiderer, wounded and in need of prompt medical attention. Only moments earlier, the sniper had put Stephen Tschiderer's heart between the crosshairs of a scope and pulled the trigger. Tschiderer could have roughed him up. He could have walked away. Instead, Tschiderer treated the wounds of his enemy.

I'm wondering where in your life God is calling you into submission, that is, voluntary selflessness? Maybe your sniper is an ex-spouse or a prodigal child or an alienated boss.

Right now God says, "It's time to let go." Will you repay insult with insult, or will you practice voluntary selflessness and repay evil with love?

I'm not talking about living without boundaries; rather I'm inviting you into a life that is governed by the laws of the kingdom of God. It's a better way to live. It's our opportunity to live "on earth, as it is in heaven."

1. William Barclay, *The Letters of James and Peter*, The Daily Study Bible Series (Philadelphia, Pa.: The Westminster Press, 1975), 219.

2. Brian Mansfield, "June Carter Cash, Country Music Legend, Dies," *USA Today*, May 15, 2003.

3. Warren Wiersbe, quoted in Darryl Dash, "When You Don't Like Who's in Charge," http://dashsermons.com/2006/11/when-you-dont-like-whos-in-charge-1-peter -213-17/ (accessed March 18, 2010).

4. James Prichard, "Michigan Man in Wheelchair Takes Wild Ride After Getting Lodged to Truck's Front Grille," Associated Press, June 8, 2007.

Chapter 7

SUFFERING, PART 1

―――

1 Peter 3:10–22

Pastor Bob Beasley of Gregory Drive Alliance Church in Ontario, Canada, tells the following story about a family in his congregation:

> Our three-year-old daughter, Rena, sat with us during the baptismal service last Sunday night, which was a new experience for her. She exclaimed in surprise, "Why he pushed that guy in the water? Why, Dad, why?" My wife tried to explain briefly and quietly, but Rena just wouldn't be satisfied. Later that night we tried to provide an answer that a child's mind could comprehend. We talked about sin and told Rena that when people decide to live for Jesus and "do good" they want everyone to know. We then explained that water symbolizes Jesus' washing people from sin; when they come out "clean," they are going to try to be "good."
>
> A moment later, we realized we'd have to work on our explanation a bit. Rena responded, "Why didn't Pastor Bob just spank him?"[1]

Well, I suppose there are different motivators for doing good, right? Peter keeps reminding us to "do good." Now he quotes from Psalm 34 and speaks of the blessing we receive from God when we "do good."

"Whoever would love life
    and see good days
must keep his tongue from evil

61

and his lips from deceitful speech.
He must turn from evil and *do good;*
   he must seek peace and pursue it.
For the eyes of the Lord are on the righteous
   and his ears are attentive to their prayer,
but the face of the Lord is against those who do evil" (1 Peter 3:10–12,
   emphasis supplied).

Peter then asks the rhetorical question, "Who is going to harm you if you are eager to do good?" Next, Peter pens this classic verse in Scripture: "But even if you should suffer for what is right, you are blessed" (verses 13, 14).

THE SOURCE OF BLESSING

It's an intriguing concept, isn't it? The life of blessing comes from suffering for what is right. I like the way author Alan Redpath expresses this idea. He writes,

> There is nothing, no circumstance, no trouble, no testing, that can ever touch me until, first of all, it has gone past God and Christ, right through to me. If it has come that far, it has come with a great purpose which I may not understand at the moment, but as I refuse to become panicky, as I lift up my eyes to Him and accept it as coming from the throne of God for some great purpose of blessing to my own heart, no sorrow will ever disturb me, . . . for I shall rest in the joy of what my Lord is.[2]

This is a great principle of spiritual life: when you endure suffering by completely trusting that God has in mind for you "some great purpose of blessing," you begin to enter into an experience with God that is truly supernatural. It is then that you can "rest in the joy of what [our] Lord is."

"Suffer for what is right and you are blessed," Peter tells the persecuted Christians of his day. Then he writes, " 'Do not fear what they fear; do not be frightened.' But in your hearts set apart Christ as Lord" (verse 15).

Basil of Caesarea, one of the Church Fathers, probably read this verse in 1 Peter; he certainly lived the text. In A.D. 370, he became the archbishop of Caesarea. This brought him into conflict with the Arian emperor Valens. In an attempt to intimidate the stubborn bishop, Valens sent the chief of his imperial guard, Modestus, to threaten him with punishment. Basil assured Modestus that he was ready and eager to die for Christ, and that he had so few possessions that banishment, confiscation, or imprisonment would mean nothing to him.

When Modestus replied that no one ever talked to him like that, Basil answered that perhaps he'd never met a bishop before. He said, "When the interests of God are at stake, we care for nothing else."

In Basil of Caesarea we see a snapshot of what Peter was calling us to when he said, "Do not fear; but in your hearts make Christ your Lord."

THE RESULT OF SUFFERING

Next, Peter writes, "Always be prepared to give an answer to everyone who asks you to give the reason for the hope that you have. But do this with gentleness and respect, keeping a clear conscience, so that those who speak maliciously against your good behavior in Christ may be ashamed of their slander" (verses 15, 16).

I like the way Eugene Peterson packages Peter's advice. *The Message* translation puts verse 16 like this, "Keep a clear conscience before God so that when people throw mud at you, none of it will stick. They'll end up realizing that they're the ones who need a bath."

Peter then concludes, "It is better, if it is God's will, to suffer for doing good than for doing evil" (verse 17).

That's good counsel when you find yourself in a season of suffering. Hardships are worthwhile when the result is "doing good" rather than "doing evil."

God's primary motive is not to carve out for you a cushy life devoid of pain. J. I. Packer was right when he said, "It needs to be said loud and clear that in the kingdom of God there ain't no comfort zone and never will be."[3] God's primary goal is not to protect you from all whitewater; rather it is to see your character transformed through the storm. Listen to Philip Yancey,

> For whatever reason, God has let this broken world endure in its fallen state for a very long time. For those of us who live in that broken world, God seems to value character more than our comfort, often using the very elements that cause us most discomfort as his tools in fashioning that character. A story is being written, with an ending only faintly glimpsed by us. We face the choice of trusting the Author along the way or striking out alone. Always, we have the choice.[4]

YOUR RESPONSE TO SUFFERING

In the end, it's your choice. How will you respond to suffering? Will you choose good or evil? Character or comfort?

At the age of twenty-five, Lance Armstrong was diagnosed with advanced testicular cancer. Following months of chemotherapy, Lance ate Mexican food, played golf, and lay on the couch. That's when his wife said, "You need to decide something: Are you going to be a golf-playing, beer-drinking, Mexican-food-eating slob for the rest of your life?"

Lance comments, "This conversation changed everything. Within days I was back on my bicycle. For the first time in my life, I rode with real strength and stamina and purpose. . . . [Cancer] taught me how to train and to win more purposefully. Pain and loss are great enhancers."[5]

Lance's story of suffering pales in comparison to how our Savior, Jesus Christ, suffered on the cross. The apostle Peter uses Jesus as an example when he speaks of surviving pain. Remember how Peter made the claim that we are blessed when we suffer for what is right? He goes on now to offer the quintessential example of purpose born out of pain by pointing to Christ on the cross.

First Peter 3:18 says, "For Christ died for sins once for all, the righteous for the unrighteous, to bring you to God." Peter's language here suggests that Christ's sacrifice was not like the sacrifices in the Old Testament where the ritual was done over and over. No, He died only once. Why? Peter says it was to bring us to God.

In the courts of ancient kings, one of the regal staff was a man called "the giver of access." This man's job was to escort people into the throne room of the king. It was a prestigious position; after all, this man decided who would get an audience with the king and who would get the slammed door. If you were not personal friends with this guardian, then usually a bribe was required in order to gain access to the king. Peter picks up on the custom of his day and claims that Jesus is the Giver of Access into the throne room of God.

Peter continues, "[Jesus] was put to death in the body but made alive by the Spirit" (verse 18).

In his novel, *A Connecticut Yankee in King Arthur's Court,* Mark Twain tells the story of an ordinary man (the Connecticut yankee) from the nineteenth century. This man is transported back to the medieval world of King Arthur. At one point he talks King Arthur into dressing like a peasant to take a journey through his kingdom. The king is completely oblivious to life in the trenches as he tries to carry on with all the pomp of the court.

In the chapter titled "The Smallpox Hut," the king and his companion happen upon a beggar's hovel. The husband lies dead, and the wife tries to warn them away, "For the fear of God, who visits with misery and death such as be harmless, tarry not here, but fly! This place is under his curse."

The king insists, "Let me come in and help you—you are sick and in trouble."

The woman asks the king to go into the loft and check on their child.

"It was a desperate place for him to be in, and might cost him his life," observes the yankee, "but it was no use to argue with him."

The king climbs a ladder looking for the girl. Twain describes the scene:

> There was a slight noise from the direction of the dim corner where the ladder was. It was the king descending. I could see that he was bearing something in one arm, and assisting himself with the other. He came forward into the light; upon his breast lay a slender girl of fifteen. She was but half conscious; she was dying of smallpox. Here was heroism at its last and loftiest possibility, its utmost summit; this was challenging death in the open field unarmed, with all the odds against the challenger, no reward set upon the contest, and no admiring world in silks and cloth-of-gold to gaze and applaud; and yet the king's bearing was as serenely brave as it had always been in those cheaper contests where knight meets knight in equal fight and clothed in protecting steel. He was great now; sublimely great. The rude statues of his ancestors in his palace should have an addition—I would see to that; and it would not be a mailed king killing a giant or a dragon, like the rest. It would be a king in commoner's garb bearing death in his arms.[6]

Such is the story of Jesus on the cross—the King in commoner's garb bearing our death in His arms.

JESUS' TRIUMPH OVER SUFFERING

Peter says,

> For Christ died for sins once for all, the righteous for the unrighteous, to bring you to God. He was put to death in the body but made alive by the Spirit, through whom also he went and preached to the spirits in prison who disobeyed long ago when God waited patiently in the days of Noah while the ark was being built. In it only a few people, eight in all, were saved through water, and this water symbolizes baptism that now saves you also—not the removal of dirt from the body but the pledge of a good conscience toward God. It saves you by the resurrection of Jesus

Christ, who has gone into heaven and is at God's right hand—with angels, authorities and powers in submission to him (verses 18–22).

Referring to this passage, Martin Luther once said, "This is a more wonderful text and a darker saying than almost any in the New Testament, so that I do not rightly know what St. Peter means."

What did Peter mean when he wrote this passage? What should we make of all this talk about Jesus preaching to the spirits in prison? And what does he mean about the removal of dirt from the body and a clean conscience?

Let's unpack it. First, Peter points out that Jesus was "put to death in the body but made alive by the Spirit"—this is clearly a reference to the Cross. Then Peter writes, "through whom also he went and preached to the spirits in prison who disobeyed long ago when God waited patiently in the days of Noah while the ark was being built."

While there are, of course, varying interpretations of this verse, it's important to remember that Peter is writing to persecuted believers who are in the midst of suffering. This ultimate conquest of a resurrected Christ over all evil would be a welcomed message of great hope to the battered believers.

In 2 Peter 2, we find similar imagery. Peter writes this,

> For if God did not spare angels when they sinned, but sent them to hell, putting them into gloomy dungeons to be held for judgment; if he did not spare the ancient world when he brought the flood on its ungodly people, but protected Noah, a preacher of righteousness, and seven others; if he condemned the cities of Sodom and Gomorrah by burning them to ashes, and made them an example of what is going to happen to the ungodly; and if he rescued Lot, a righteous man . . . then the Lord knows how to rescue godly men from trials and to hold the unrighteous for the day of judgment, while continuing their punishment (verses 4–9).

Peter wants to be sure that we understand that God will ultimately triumph over Satan. God will punish the unjust and deliver us from evil.

Just as the ark is a symbol of salvation for the godly in Noah's day, so baptism is a symbol of salvation for us today. Peter tells us that in Noah's day, eight people "were saved through water, and this water symbolizes baptism that now saves you also—not the removal of dirt from the body but the pledge of a good conscience toward God. It saves you by the resurrection of

Jesus Christ, who has gone into heaven and is at God's right hand—with angels, authorities and powers in submission to him" (1 Peter 3:20–22).

Note that we're not saved by being baptized; we are saved by our resurrected Savior, Jesus Christ. Baptism is simply an expression of an internal reality that we have accepted salvation in Christ. The result of baptism, according to Peter, is more than just removing external dirt from the body. Baptism is about an internal cleansing, about a "good conscience toward God."

Pat Summerall, the popular sports announcer, tells of the significance of baptism in his life. In his late sixties he overcame alcoholism and accepted Christ as his Savior. He remembers his baptism like this: "I went down in the water, and when I came up it was like a 40-pound weight had been lifted from me. I have a happier life, a healthy life, and a more positive feeling about life than ever before."[7]

You, too, can feel happy, clean, forgiven. No matter how much you have suffered or what you have done or where you have been, Jesus will forgive you. He died on the cross and was resurrected in order to have the authority to make you clean again.

Perhaps you have not been baptized. It's never too late. In November 2005, Yahoo!News reported the story of Ivy Smith, who was baptized for the first time. She was 101 years old![8]

If you haven't already, let me encourage you to find a Bible-based church in your community. Talk to the pastor and be baptized. Or perhaps for you it would be a rebaptism. Whatever your story, wouldn't you love to feel clean before God?

1. As quoted from http://preachingtoday.com/illustrations/article_print.html?id=23632.

2. Alan Redpath "God's Purpose in Difficult Times," Julie Bergeron Studios (accessed March 9, 2010).

3. J. I. Packer, "We Can Overcome," *Christianity Today,* October 2, 2000.

4. Philip Yancey, *Reaching for the Invisible God* (Grand Rapids, Mich.: Zondervan, 2000), 284.

5. Lance Armstrong, "Back in the Saddle," *Forbes,* December 3, 2001.

6. Mark Twain, "The Smallpox Hunt," *A Connecticut Yankee in King Arthur's Court.*

7. Art Stricklin, *Sports Spectrum,* November/December, 2001, 27.

8. "British Churchgoer Waits 101 Years to be Baptized," *Yahoo!News,* November 17, 2005.

Chapter 8

STRANGENESS

---

1 Peter 4:1–11

In his book *Is It Real When It Doesn't Work?* Doug Murren, a pastor in the Foursquare denomination, tells the following story:

> I grew up a redhead (still am). I was the kid you could always spot in a crowd. On a nice Saturday afternoon, about six of us kids, including one who owned a BB gun, were shooting the smithereens out of the stained-glass window of a Seventh-day Adventist Church behind my parents' house. It was not only great fun, but also great target practice. One section had just about been knocked out when the custodian came charging out of the church.
>
> We all ran like the dickens. We jumped over the fence, ran home, and acted as though everything were cool and normal. The only problem was that when the police asked the custodian who had broken the window, he remembered seeing a redheaded kid. Of course, when the police questioned the neighbors about a redheaded kid who lived close to the church, their trail led right to our doorstep.
>
> Thankfully I didn't own a gun and hadn't shot out any of the windows myself. I had simply been an enthusiastic spectator. The culprit who did own the gun ended up paying for the window.
>
> In a very real sense, when you become a Christian, God turns you into a redhead too. You stick out in a crowd.[1]

That's what the apostle Peter tells Christians in 1 Peter 4. He describes the culture as full of "debauchery, lust, drunkenness, orgies, carousing and detestable idolatry." Peter continues, "They think it strange that you do not plunge with them into the same flood of dissipation" (verses 3, 4). Peter reminds us as Christians that we are strangers in this world. We live counter to the pagan culture of our day. We don't fit into the value system of this world.

As someone observed, "The ship's place is in the sea, but God pity the ship when the sea gets into it. The Christian's place is in the world, but God pity the Christian if the world gets the best of him."[2]

We are called to be strangers in this world. A. W. Tozer, that leathery saint of yesteryear, once commented on our strangeness,

> A real Christian is an odd number anyway. He feels supreme love for One whom he has never seen, talks familiarly every day to Someone he cannot see, expects to go to heaven on the virtue of Another, empties himself in order to be full, admits he is wrong so he can be declared right, goes down in order to get up, is strong when he is weakest, richest when he is poorest, and happiest when he feels worst. He dies so he can live, forsakes in order to have, gives away so he can keep, sees the invisible, hears the inaudible, and knows that which passeth knowledge.[3]

Eugene Peterson translates the verses that follow (1 Peter 4:4–6) in this way,

> Of course, your old friends don't understand why you don't join in with the old gang anymore. But you don't have to give an account to them. They're the ones who will be called on the carpet—and before God himself. Listen to the Message. It was preached to those believers who are now dead, and yet even though they died (just as all people must), they will still get in on the life that God has given in Jesus (*The Message*).

LISTEN UP

There is a ring of urgency in Peter's voice now. He commands, "Listen to the Message." He then reminds believers that they will receive the eternal life that God has given in Jesus. As Christians, we must not follow the standards of this world. Remember that we are strangers here. If we are not countercultural, we are not Christian. Our allegiance belongs to Jesus Christ, who is soon to return to this earth and claim His own.

Peter says that when you see the "debauchery, lust, drunkenness, orgies, carousing and detestable idolatry" in this world you can know this, "The end of all things is near" (verses 3, 7).

Jesus is coming again! Ours is a dark and evil world, but don't despair, Jesus is coming again. So what are we to do as we wait for the second coming of Christ? Peter answers that question. He calls us to do three things.

1. PRAY.

First, he writes, "Therefore be clear minded and self-controlled so that you can pray" (verse 7).

On June 8, 2009, Emma Daniel Gray died at the age of ninty-five. The *Washington Post* carried a story about her because for twenty-four years she cleaned the office of the President of the United States. She served six presidents before she retired in 1979. Her official title? Charwoman.

What made Mrs. Gray's story and her life newsworthy was her custom to pray. She would stand and pray over the president's chair each time she dusted it—her cleaning supplies in one hand, the other on the chair. She'd pray for blessings, wisdom, and safety.

While reflecting on the way she lived, her pastor said, "She saw life through the eyes of promise is the way I'd put it. You can always look around and find reasons to be [unhappy] . . . but you couldn't be around her and not know what she believed."

As we wait for the imminent return of Jesus, we too are called to see life through the eyes of promise—and pray accordingly.[4]

2. LOVE.

Secondly, we can love. "Above all," Peter writes, "love each other deeply, because love covers over a multitude of sins" (verse 8).

As we wait for Jesus to come, we are called to love each other. Whether Jesus comes before or after you die is irrelevant; what really matters is that you seize every opportunity to carry out God's one and all-consuming command—love each other.

Perhaps you remember the news story of Kelly James. He was the forty-eight-year-old landscape architect who loved climbing mountains. On December 9, 2006, he and two of his friends climbed Mount Hood in Oregon. Tragically, they were assailed by a sudden blizzard after scaling the summit and took refuge in a snow cave. Kelly used his cell phone to call his family and tell them what was going on, but the storm was too severe for rescue workers to effect a rescue. All three hikers died.

In an interview with Katie Couric on the *CBS Evening News,* Kelly's widow, Karen James, shared of the faith in Jesus Christ that had defined life for the couple. During the interview, Couric asked if Karen was angry at all with her husband for choosing to climb in the first place. She replied, "I'm not angry. I'm really sad our journey is over, for a while, and I miss him terribly. But he loved life so much, and he taught me how to love. He taught me how to live. And I don't know how you can be angry at someone who loved their family, who loved God . . . and gave back so much more than he took."

When asked how her husband would like to be remembered, Karen again spoke of her husband's faith in Jesus, "Kelly had this little ornament, and he's had it since he was little. It's a manger. It's just this little plastic thing. And it's always the tradition that [our son] Jack and Kelly put it on the tree together. And so I said this Christmas, 'We're going to put that ornament on the tree.' And one of the things that we really understand about Christmas is that little baby born in a barn is the reason our family has so much strength now."

Impressed by the strength of Karen's faith, Couric asked if the family's confidence in God had been tested by her husband's death. "No, it was never tested," Karen answered. "I remember one time we were watching TV, and Kelly said to me, 'I can't wait to go to heaven.' And I said, 'What?' We were watching some show that had nothing to do with it. And he said, 'Yeah, that's going to be really cool.' "

To conclude, Couric asked if there were any lessons that could be learned from her husband's tragedy. Karen replied, "I've told a colleague of mine that men should hold their wives really, really tight, because you don't know when our journey's going to end. My journey ended with an 'I love you.' And . . . for others, if their journey ends with an 'I love you,' it's a lot to hold onto."[5]

Whether by death or by the Second Coming—however your journey on this earth ends—may it be with an "I love you." "Love each other deeply."

3. SERVE.

Finally, Peter calls us to serve. "Offer hospitality to one another without grumbling. Each one should use whatever gift he has received to serve others, faithfully administering God's grace in its various forms" (verses 9, 10).

No one knows when Jesus is coming again, but until that day, we know that God calls us to serve one another. "Every duty performed," Ellen White reminds us, "every sacrifice made in the name of Jesus, brings an exceeding great reward. In the very act of duty, God speaks and gives His blessing."[6]

Bettye Tucker offers a wonderful snapshot of what Christians should be doing as we wait for Jesus to come. A 2009 article in the *Chicago Tribune* told the story of this woman who works as the night-shift cook at Children's Memorial Hospital in Chicago, Illinois. For forty-three years (twenty-eight of them on the night shift) she has been faithfully performing her job. She sees a lot of parents in her job, many of them frightened and weary. On one evening around the time the article was written, Miss Bettye (as she is called by all her friends) served food to a mother whose three-year-old fell out of a second story window that morning, another mother whose seventeen-year-old was battling a rare form of leukemia, and a third mother whose eighteen-year-old had endured seven hours of brain surgery. Their stories break Miss Bettye's heart, and—as one coworker interviewed for the article says— "that's why she feeds every last one of them as if they had walked right into the 'too-small' kitchen of [the] South Side brick bungalow [where she lives]." A member of the hospital's housekeeping crew says of Miss Bettye, "You need someone to bring you life, and she brings it in the middle of the night."

The article includes a picture of Miss Bettye modeling her thousand-watt smile. One can only imagine how much that smile would mean to a suffering parent or child. She says, "When I ask, 'How you doin' today?' and they say it's not a good day, I say, 'Don't lose hope.' When the nurses tell me it's a bad night, I say, 'I understand it's a bad night. But guess what? I am here for you. I'm going to get you through the night.' "

Another picture shows Bettye sitting down, head bowed, over a meal. "I'm a praying lady," she says in the article. "I pray every night, for every room and every person in the hospital. I start with the basement, and I go up, floor by floor, room by room. I pray for the children, I pray for the families, I pray for the nurses and the doctors. . . . I say, every night while I'm driving in on the expressway, 'Oh, Lord, I don't know what I'll face tonight, but I pray you'll guide me through.' "[7]

Jesus is coming again. But for today, take a page out of Miss Bettye's playbook. Cook up some compassion. Pray, love, and serve . . . until He comes.

1. Doug Murren and Barb Shurin, *Is It Real When It Doesn't Work?* (Nashville, Tenn.: Thomas Nelson Publishers, 1990), 206, 207.

2. S. Rickly Christian, *Alive 2* (Grand Rapids, Mich.: Zondervan Publishing House, 1990), 157.

3. A. W. Tozer quoted in Wil Pounds, "Christ in You, the Hope of Glory," http://www.abideinchrist.com/messages/col1v27.html (accessed March 9, 2010).

4. Patricia Sullivan, " 'Christian Lady' Cleaned for 6 Presidents," *The Washington Post,* June 21, 2009 http://www.washingtonpost.com/wp-dyn/content/article/2009/06/20/AR2009062001661.html (accessed March 9, 2009).

5. Melissa McNamara, "Climber's Widow Tells Her Story," *CBS Evening News,* December 22, 2006, http://www.cbsnews.com/stories/2006/12/21/eveningnews/main2291454.shtml (accessed March 9, 2010).

6. Ellen White, *Testimonies for the Church,* vol. 4 (Mountain View, Calif.: Pacific Press® Publishing Association, 1948), 145.

7. Barbara Mahany, "Cook. Pray. Love: Bettye Tucker Helps the Kids and the Caregivers Make It Through the Night at Children's Memorial," *Chicago Tribune,* September 19, 2009, section 6, http://archives.chicagotribune.com/2009/sep/19/health/chi-0920-sun-nightcook (accessed March 9, 2010).

Chapter 9

SUFFERING, PART 2

---

1 Peter 4:12–19

"The answer to suffering cannot just be an abstract idea, because this isn't an abstract issue; it's a personal issue," claims Dr. Peter J. Kreeft. "It requires a personal response. It's not a bunch of words, it's *the* Word. It's not a tightly woven philosophical argument; it's a person. *The* person. The answer must be someone, not just something, because the issue involves someone— *God, where are You?*"[1]

It's a fair question, isn't it? Perhaps you've asked it yourself, "God, where are You?"

No doubt many Christians asked that question in the first century when they were hiding in caves for fear of being persecuted by the lunatic emperor, Nero. So Peter pens a letter addressed to these battered Christians to say, "Don't be discouraged in your suffering. Don't be surprised when you face painful trials. God never promised a cushy ride in life."

Dr. Paul Cedar, in his commentary on 1 Peter, writes, "Many Christians are surprised or shocked when the trials and sufferings of Christ come into their lives. There is a popular theology which is espoused by some which suggests that the sun always shines upon the Christians, that our grass is always green, and that the spiritual temperature around us is always ideal. Peter is reminding us that such teaching is simply not true."[2]

First Peter 4:12–14 says this, "Dear friends, do not be surprised at the painful trial you are suffering, as though something strange were happening to you. But rejoice that you participate in the sufferings of Christ, so that you may be overjoyed when his glory is revealed. If you are insulted because of the name of Christ, you are blessed, for the Spirit of glory and of God rests on you."

Phillip Yancey has been helpful to me on this sticky subject of suffering and pain. He writes,

> I once was part of a small group with a Christian leader whose name you would likely recognize. He went through a hard time as his adult children got into trouble, bringing him sleepless nights and expensive attorney fees. Worse, my friend was diagnosed with a rare form of cancer. Nothing in his life seemed to work out.
>
> "I have no problem believing in a good God," he said to us one night. "My question is, 'What is God good for?' "
>
> We listened to his complaints and tried various responses, but he batted them all away. A few weeks later, I came across a little phrase by Dallas Willard: "For those who love God, nothing irredeemable can happen to you." I went back to my friend.
>
> "What about that?" I asked. "Is God good for that promise?"[3]

I believe He is good for that promise. Everything in life—good or bad—is redeemable by God. Peter claims, "the painful trial you are suffering" will result in the "blessed" life.

In the next two verses, Peter goes on to say, "If you suffer, it should not be as a murderer or thief or any other kind of criminal, or even as a meddler. However, if you suffer as a Christian, do not be ashamed, but praise God that you bear that name" (verses 15, 16).

Peter brings the words of Jesus to mind, "Blessed are you when people insult you, persecute you and falsely say all kinds of evil against you because of me" (Matthew 5:11).

There is no shame in suffering for being a Christian. When Peter and John were persecuted for preaching the gospel, they rejoiced because persecution showed God's approval of their work (see Acts 5:41). "Don't seek out suffering, and don't try to avoid it. Instead, keep on doing what is right regardless of the suffering it might bring."[4]

Then Peter writes, "For it is time for judgment to begin with the family of God; and if it begins with us, what will the outcome be for those who do not obey the gospel of God? And, 'If it is hard for the righteous to be saved, what will become of the ungodly and the sinner?' " (1 Peter 4:17, 18).

I. Howard Marshall offers this commentary, "Christians need to take the judgment of God seriously. From the grim experiences of believers, however, one can draw the conclusion that the judgment on those who actively reject the gospel and oppose believers will be all the more grim. The sufferings of Christians are mild by comparison."[5]

Peter continues, "So then, those who suffer according to God's will should commit themselves to their faithful Creator and continue to do good" (verse 19).

Peter revisits one of his favorite themes in this letter to remind us that even in suffering we must "do good." If we suffer as a consequence of our foolish choices—such as thievery, meddling, or any criminal behavior—then there is no honor in that. Ah, but if we suffer as a consequence of keeping God's will—and we "do good" as a result—then we will be rewarded with eternal life on the day of judgment.

Dr. Condoleezza Rice, during the time she served as the U. S. National Security Advisor, shared this insightful perspective at the National Prayer Breakfast shortly after the tragedies of September 11:

> We are living through a time of testing and consequence—and praying that our wisdom and will are equal to the work before us. And it is at times like these that we are reminded of a paradox, that it is a privilege to struggle. A privilege to struggle for what is right and true. A privilege to struggle for freedom over tyranny. A privilege, even, to struggle with the most difficult and profound moral choices.
>
> American slaves used to sing, "Nobody knows the trouble I've seen—Glory Hallelujah!" Growing up, I would often wonder at the seeming contradiction contained in this line. But as I grew older, I came to learn that there is no contradiction at all.
>
> I believe this same message is found in the Bible in Romans 5, where we are told to "rejoice in our sufferings, knowing that suffering produces endurance, and endurance produces character, and character produces hope, and hope does not disappoint us, because God's love has been poured into our hearts through the Holy Spirit which has been given to us."[6]

Dr. Rice went on to highlight two important lessons. "First," she said, "there is the lesson that only through struggle do we realize the depths of our resilience and understand that the hardest of blows can be survived and overcome. . . . It is through struggle that we find redemption and self-knowledge. In this sense it is a privilege to struggle."

Dr. Rice continued by highlighting Peter's point about the redemptive value of suffering when it results in good. "There is a second, more important, lesson to be learned from struggle and suffering. . . . We can use the strength it gives us for the good of others. Nothing good is born of personal struggle if it is used to fuel one's sense of entitlement, or superiority to those who we perceive to have struggled less than we."[7]

She concluded by saying, "If terror and tragedy spur us to rediscover and strengthen these commitments, then we can truly say that some good has come from great loss. And in all the trials that may lie ahead, we will carry these commitments close to our heart so we may leave a better world for those who follow. This is our prayer for our Nation and our people. This is our prayer for all Nations and all peoples. Lord, hear our prayer."[8]

1. Lee Strobel, *The Case for Faith* (Grand Rapids, Mich.: Zondervan Publishing House, 2000).

2. Paul A. Cedar, *James, 1, 2 Peter, Jude,* The Communicator's Commentary (Waco, Tex.: Word Books, 1984), 184.

3. Philip Yancey, "Where Is God When It Hurts?" *Christianity Today,* June 2007, 56.

4. *Life Application Bible,* New International Version (Wheaton, Ill.: Tyndale House Publishers, 1999), 2264.

5. I. Howard Marshall, *1 Peter* (Downers Grove, Ill.: InterVarsity Press, 1991), 156, 157.

6. "Remarks by National Security Advisor, Dr. Condoleezza Rice, at the National Prayer Breakfast," February 6, 2002, Washington Hilton Hotel, Washington, D.C., http://www.aarlc.org/news/condiremarks.shtml (accessed March 9, 2010).

7. Ibid.

8. Ibid.

Chapter 10

SERVING

---

1 Peter 5:1–7

In 1970 at the age of sixty-six, Robert Greenleaf published "The Servant as Leader," the first of a dozen essays and books on servant leadership. Since that time, more than a half-million copies of his books and essays have been sold worldwide.

Still today, occasionally you find business leaders like Marlo Boux who strive to put Greanleaf's philosophy into practice by leading through serving. A November 5, 2005, press release reports Marlo's story. She is a business consultant who discovered that thousands of moms across North America are trying to make ends meet by working from home. Many of these moms, however, could never afford the services of a much-needed coach.

The press release contains this quotation by Marlo:

> During my coach training, it was repeatedly stated that you should never compromise your asking price with a client. The idea being that doing so would devalue your services. When I initially set up my fee schedule, I kept these business principles in mind and determined my fees according to my educational background, experience, and the cost of doing business alone. I didn't anticipate so many women working from home. . . . These women were in no position financially to afford a coach. One evening I awoke at 4:00 A.M. to attend to my infant daughter and Holy Spirit had a message for me: your job is to advance God's Kingdom by supporting moms working from home, leave the bottom line to me.[1]

In obedience to God, Marlo changed her business strategy. If her clients can't afford her suggested fees, then she works for free. She explains, "Jesus wasn't an elitist—He was a servant leader. His message is for all who will listen and embrace it. He uses ordinary people like me to advance His Kingdom every day. I want to be a part of that."

That's a radical business plan, isn't it? "You set your own price. I'm just here to serve you." Imagine the local Cadillac dealer modeling that plan— "whatever you want to pay for the Escalade is fine."

Marlo's business model predates Robert Greenleaf by many centuries. It's at least as old as the apostle Peter. In his letter to the first-century Christians, Peter challenges us to practice the principles of servant leadership. You may recall 1 Peter 3 where Peter addresses wives, then husbands; then he speaks to all who would claim the name of Christ. Peter follows a similar format in this passage. He speaks first to the elders, then to the young, then to all of us. Notice first what he has to say to the elders of the church.

1. THE ELDERS.

"To the elders among you, I appeal as a fellow elder, a witness of Christ's sufferings and one who also will share in the glory to be revealed" (1 Peter 5:1).

Peter alludes to the sufferings of Christ and claims that he himself is a witness to this pain. This is a reminder to all who would lead—particularly in the church—that there is a price to be paid. Servant leadership is not for wimps.

I've heard of a preacher who quit the ministry after twenty years and became a funeral director. When asked why he changed, he explained, "I spent three years trying to straighten out John, and John's still an alcoholic; then I spent six months trying to straighten out Susan's marriage, but she filed for divorce; then I spent two years trying to straighten out Bob's drug problem, and he's still an addict. Now at the funeral home when I straighten them out—they stay straight!"

The work of the church leader can be difficult at times. Peter understood this and reminds his readers that he is a witness of Christ's sufferings. But he also reminds us that to lead is to share in the glory of Christ. So he insists that elders in the church "be shepherds of God's flock that is under your care" (verse 2).

The King James Version translates it like this, "Feed the flock of God." No doubt Peter is remembering the conversation with Jesus recorded in John 21, during which Jesus asks him, "Peter, do you love Me?"

"Of course I do," Peter replies.

You remember the command then that Jesus gave? "Feed My sheep." Three times Jesus asks Peter, "Do you love Me?" Three times He commands Peter, "Then feed My sheep."

Peter passes along this command to the leaders in the church. Feed the flock of God, he says, "serving as overseers—not because you must, but because you are willing"—in other words, because you are a servant leader— "as God wants you to be; not greedy for money, but eager to serve; not lording it over those entrusted to you, but being examples to the flock. And when the Chief Shepherd appears, you will receive the crown of glory that will never fade away" (verses 2–4).

"Your reward will come," Peter assures those who will take up the cause of servant leadership. "So serve the flock."

Maybe you've heard Doug Peterson's story "The Career of Horville Sash." The tale offers a good picture of servant leadership. Horville Sash had a very humble job in the offices of the largest corporation in the world. He worked as a mail clerk in the basement of the building doing what he could to help other people with their jobs. Often he wondered what happened on the floor just above his.

One day, Horville found a bug scurrying across the floor. Before he could stomp the life out of the bug, it spoke, "Please don't kill me," said the bug. "If you let me live, I'll give you three wishes."

Horville played along—never expecting the bug to make good on the promise. The bug asked Horville what he wanted for his first wish. "To be promoted to the second floor," came the reply. The next day Horville's boss promoted him to the second floor.

Soon Horville heard footsteps on the floor above him. He said to the bug, "My second wish is to be promoted floor by floor until I reach the very top. I aspire to be CEO of the company."

"Done," said the bug, and floor by floor Horville moved north through the ranks: 10th floor, 20th floor, 50th floor, 90th floor, and finally to the very top floor, as CEO. He was as high as he could go—so he thought.

Then one day he heard footsteps above him. He saw a sign that said, STAIRS. He went up and found a rooftop and there he found one of his clerks near the edge of the building with his eyes closed.

"What are you doing?" Horville asked.

"Praying," came the answer.

"To whom?"

Pointing a finger toward the sky the young man answered, "God."

Panic gripped Horville. There was a floor above him? He couldn't see it. All he saw was clouds. He couldn't hear the shuffling of feet. "Do you mean there is an authority over me?"

Horville summoned the bug. It was time for his third and final wish. "Make me God," he demanded. "Make me the highest. Put me in the kind of position only God would hold if he were here on earth."

The next day Horville Sash awakened to find himself in the basement, sorting the mail, and doing what he could to help others be the best that they could possibly be. That's how Horville Sash learned what Jesus meant when He said, "Whoever wants to become great among you must be your servant" (Matthew 20:26).

Peter lifts up Jesus as the model for servant leadership for all the elders who would serve in the church.

2. YOUNG MEN.

Next, Peter writes, "Young men, in the same way be submissive to those who are older" (1 Peter 5:5).

Notice the phrase, "in the same way." In other words, everything that Peter has said to the overseers, or elders, applies to the young men as well. Then he adds the command, "be submissive to those who are older." Earlier we unpacked this word *submissive* when Peter called wives to be submissive to their husbands. We learned that submission is not about lording over those who are weaker or inferior. Submission is really about voluntary selflessness. It is not a position of weakness but of strength. In the same way that Christ lived a life of submission, that is, voluntary selflessness, so we, too, are called to be submissive—not out of fear or weakness, but out of choice and strength. Here, Peter specifically gives this counsel to young men.

When I was in college, I picked up a poem at a Bible conference that notched such a deep impression in my mind that twenty years later I tracked down Maria Runge, the author, for permission to reprint it in my book *Out of the Hot Tub, Into the World.* Listen to the ending of that piece:

> *If I could have another wish, only a temporary one—*
> I would turn the clock ahead for young people and make them old. Let them hobble because of stiff joints, let them walk a little slower and eat a little longer. Let them be lonely and shut in from the world, especially on holidays. Let them have only memories, but no love. Let

them be frightened by young prowlers, beaten by young thieves.

Then when they are young again, they will be more considerate of senior citizens.

If I could have just one wish, a permanent one—

I would wish that everyone would follow the second great commandment, loving his neighbor as himself, with compassion and sensitivity. Then there would be no hurts or tears, no loneliness or fear.

This last wish will come true! Jesus is coming soon.[2]

I suspect Peter would give a hearty "Amen to this challenge for young people to love and serve the older generation." He goes on then to extend this invitation to be a servant leader to everyone who would claim the name of Christ.

3. ALL OF YOU.

Verses 5 and 6 say this, "All of you, clothe yourselves with humility toward one another, because, 'God opposes the proud but gives grace to the humble.' Humble yourselves, therefore, under God's mighty hand, that he may lift you up in due time."

Peter appeals to all of us—not just to the elders and the young men, but to all of us. He calls us to lead with humility and a spirit of voluntary selflessness.

So are you up to his challenge? Whether you're the CEO of a Fortune 500 company or a stay-at-home dad, Jesus calls you to be a servant. Whether you're leading a workforce or your family, you will have plenty of opportunities today to let those around you know that you are a servant. Embrace the tasks that others shun. Notice the needs of people around you. Seek to serve. And you will be great in the only kingdom that counts.

---

1. "Christian Small Business Coach Bucks Coaching Industry Trend and Allows Clients to Determine Their Own Monthly Fees," *PR Leap,* http://www.prleap.com/pr/18642.

2. Marion Runge, "If I Could Have One Wish . . . ," *Adventist Review,* January 28, 1982.

Chapter 11

SPIRITUAL HEALTH

---

1 Peter 5 : 8 – 14

At the 1993 annual meeting of The American Heart Association, three hundred thousand doctors, nurses, and researchers met in Atlanta to discuss, among other things, the importance of a low-fat diet in keeping our hearts healthy. Yet during meal times, many of the participants wolfed down bacon cheeseburgers, French fries, and other high-fat fast food. When one cardiologist was asked whether or not his eating high-fat meals set a bad example, he replied, "Not me . . . because I took my name tag off."

While Peter does not specifically address the issue of physical health, he has been teaching us about spiritual health. Over and over we have heard the plea from his pen to live authentic lives in Christ. "If you claim the name of Christ," Peter urges, "then leave on your name tag."

CAST YOUR CARES UPON GOD

The parting challenge of his first letter offers an apt prescription for spiritual health. Consider the three parts of Peter's prescription, beginning with this one, "Cast all your anxiety on him because he cares for you" (1 Peter 5:7). To the degree that we follow Peter's prescription, we are healthier and happier. An enlarging body of research focuses on this relationship between religion and mental health. The January 17, 2005, issue of *Time* magazine reports,

Religious people are less depressed, less anxious and less suicidal than nonreligious people. And they are better able to cope with such crises as illness, divorce and bereavement. "Even if you compare two people who have symptoms of depression," says Michael McCullough, an associate professor of psychology and religious studies at the University of Miami, "the more religious person will be a little less sad."

Studies show that the more a believer incorporates religion into daily living—attending services, reading Scripture, praying—the better off he or she appears to be on two measures of happiness: frequency of positive emotions and overall sense of satisfaction with life.[1]

Consider as well the study in *Newsweek* magazine that reports how church attendance lengthens life. In studying the relationship between religion and health, researchers discovered that those who did not attend church lived an average of seventy-five years; less than weekly attendance, lived eighty years; once a week eighty-two years; and those who attended church more than once a week, lived an average of eighty-three years.[2] Now I don't care how boring your local church pastor is, surely it's worth enduring the dull sermons for an extra eight years of living, don't you think?

Science is confirming what Peter wrote long ago. The apostle prescribes the optimum life—which is only found in God.

BE SELF-CONTROLLED AND ALERT

How can you enter into this life? First, you must cast all your cares upon God. Second, Peter writes, "Be self-controlled and alert. Your enemy the devil prowls around like a roaring lion looking for someone to devour" (verse 8).

In the opening chapter, we looked at advice found in *The Worst Case Scenario Survival Handbook.* One of the chapters in this *New York Times* bestseller explains what to do if confronted by an angry lion. Do you know? According to the book, you are to make yourself look bigger by opening your coat. Well, your chances of encountering a literal lion today are quite slim. But in the spiritual realm, it's quite likely.

"The devil," Peter says, "prowls like a lion." How do we survive? "Be self-controlled and alert." Saint Francis once warned, "Be alert, therefore, for the devil, who, if he can claim even one hair of your head, will lose no time in making a braid of it."[3]

"Be careful," Peter warns, "for the devil is devious and he will destroy you."

Mel Gibson was asked why he chose a veiled female figure to portray evil in his movie *The Passion of the Christ.* He answered, Because evil "takes on the form of beauty. It is almost beautiful. It is the great aper of God. But the mask is askew; there is always something wrong. Evil masquerades, but if your antennae are up, you'll detect it."[4]

To be spiritually healthy, Peter calls us to keep the antennae up. Be careful. Dropping your spiritual guard will spell your demise.

In 2004, the Boston Public Library opened an exhibit to commemorate the eighty-fifth anniversary of the Great Molasses Flood. This tragedy killed 21 people and injured 150. On January 15, 1919, an enormous steel vat, containing 2.3 million gallons of molten molasses, burst. Tidal waves of syrup—thirty feet tall—destroyed buildings, crushed freight cars and automobiles, and drowned people. Some referred to it as the "Dark Tide."

What caused it? The holding tank, 50 feet high and 240 feet around, had constant leaks. To address the problem, they repainted the tank to match the color of the leaking molasses![5] It was only a matter of time until disaster struck.

I'm wondering: Are you painting over any hazardous situations in your life? Maybe it's visiting Internet sites that imperil your soul. Perhaps you're taking ethical shortcuts in the workplace. It could be that you're investing a lot of time in a relationship that you know does not honor God. Whatever it is, stop! Be alert.

Nobody takes that first sip of booze hoping to murder an innocent victim while driving under the influence; and yet every DUI fatality begins with one sip from someone who thinks, *It could never happen to me. I can handle my liquor.* No woman flirts with her boss thinking that it will destroy her family; and yet that's how affairs often begin. Nobody cheats on their income tax thinking they'll land in jail; and yet that's where it starts. The destruction of one's soul begins with small compromises in the mind of someone who thinks, *I can handle the devil's temptations.* Oh no you can't! You must flee temptation, and don't leave a forwarding address. The devil is too cunning; you cannot match spiritual wits with Satan.

RESIST THE DEVIL

Peter then gives one more prescription. In the next verse he says, "Resist [the devil], standing firm in the faith, because you know that your brothers throughout the world are undergoing the same kind of sufferings" (verse 9).

Frankly, I find this to be a refreshing, in-your-face challenge to take responsibility in a world in which it seems no one really wants to be responsible for their actions. Just look at the proliferation of lawsuits in our country. We're so quick to blame others—and then we expect to be compensated for it.

You probably know about some of the crazy suits that clog up our courts. For example, Judith Haimes, a psychic from Philadelphia, was awarded $986,000 when she claimed that a CT scan ordered by a physician impaired her psychic abilities. Now if she was psychic, shouldn't she have known not to go to that doctor? It's a crazy world where we so often want to shirk responsibility and blame others for our problems.

Peter doesn't play that game. Instead, he calls us to take responsibility for our own spiritual health and to resist the devil. The key question is "How?" How do we resist the devil? A clear answer comes from the book of James, "Submit yourselves, then, to God. Resist the devil, and he will flee from you" (James 4:7). The *only* way to resist the devil is to submit yourself to God.

An old priest was asked by a young man, "Father, when will I cease to be bothered by the temptations of the flesh?"

The priest replied, "I wouldn't trust myself, son, until I was dead for three days."

Here's the bottom line: you can't trust yourself to triumph over temptation. The devil is too strong. The only way to resist the devil, according to James, is to submit yourself to God.

We learn this lesson from the cuckoo bird. What's interesting about this bird is that it never builds its own nest. When momma bird feels an egg coming on, she finds an unguarded nest with eggs. The cuckoo lands, hurriedly lays its egg, and takes off again. That's all the cuckoo does in terms of parenting.

Let's say it's a thrush whose nest has been invaded. Being mathematically challenged, momma thrush fails to notice the extra egg. Four little thrushes and one large cuckoo eventually hatch. But the cuckoo is two or three times the size of the thrushes.

Mrs. Thrush, having hatched the five little birds, goes off early in the morning to get the worm. She comes back, circles the nest to see four little thrush mouths and one cavernous cuckoo mouth. Who gets the worm? The cuckoo.

So the cuckoo gets bigger and bigger and the thrushes get smaller and smaller. To find a baby cuckoo in a nest, simply look for little dead thrushes on the ground. The cuckoo discards them as they die. The adult thrush keeps feeding the baby cuckoo—even though it is three times as big as the thrush.

You and I have two natures in one nest. The nature you feed will grow, and the nature you starve will diminish. That's how you resist the devil. Submit to God. This means that you seek to feed the spiritual nature through the regular practice of the spiritual disciplines. By living in the presence of God, through prayer, Bible study, worship, service, fasting, and so on, you feed that spiritual nature and starve the carnal nature. God then begins to live in you and me and His holiness pervades our lives.[6]

Over and over Peter has called us to live according to the value system of the kingdom of God. Two dominions are at work on this earth—the dominion of the devil and the dominion of the Divine. You have to choose. Will you build your life on the Rock (that is, the Cornerstone who is Christ) or on sand?

It's decision time. Will the words of Peter be just words, or will you take these words to heart and craft a life that is built upon the value system of God's kingdom? Will you invest your time, your finances, your talents into the kingdom of our Savior or into the kingdom of self? Will you repent of your sins and accept the full forgiveness of Jesus Christ? You must decide.

The bad news is this: We have all fallen victim to the tactics of the evil one prowling about, seeking to devour every follower of Jesus. Moreover, should we shun the invitation of Jesus, we have no hope of spiritual victory or eternal life. The good news, however, reminds us that when we repent of our sins and accept the gift of Jesus on the cross, we are clean and forgiven— as if we had never sinned!

Author and pastor Gordon MacDonald illustrates by thinking about the day that Jesus was baptized. The masses were pressed to make a decision for or against God. MacDonald imagines someone organizing the baptismal candidates on that day by setting up a table with name tags and markers. In an attempt to be more personal, the secretary instructs, "Just step forward, and tell us your first name and your most awful sin."

Up to this table steps Bob. "Name?"

"Bob."

"What's your most awful sin, Bob?"

"I stole some money from my boss once." The secretary takes a marker and writes, BOB: EMBEZZLER.

Next person: "Name?"

"Mary."

"Mary, what's your most awful sin?"

"I slandered some people. I said things that weren't true. I just didn't like them." So the secretary writes, MARY: SLANDERER.

"Name?"

"George."

"What's your most awful sin?"

"I've been coveting my neighbor's Corvette." GEORGE: COVETER

"Name?"

"Gordon."

"Gordon, your most awful sin?"

"Adultery." GORDON: ADULTERER.

The secretary, with some degree of gloating, slaps the name tag on the chest of each person. Then all these people, with their name tags and their most awful sins, line up by the river, waiting to be baptized.

Up to the table comes Jesus. Jesus' most awful sin? Well, there isn't one. Literally—there is not *one* sin. So Jesus starts walking down the line. He steps up to Bob and says, "Bob, give me your name tag," and He puts it on Himself. "Mary, give Me your name tag." He puts it on Himself. "George, give Me your name tag." It goes on Himself. "Gordon, give Me your name tag."

Soon the Son of God resembles a mummy—covered with name tags and awful sins. Someone comes up and gently says to Jesus, "It's a nice thing You're doing. If You must do this, couldn't You take off a few of the worst ones? If You're going to spawn a Messianic movement, You've got to be above reproach. Why don't You take off the tag that says, MURDERER. Take the ADULTERER tag off too. Those are too despicable. We're talking about nines and tens here."

Jesus says, "You don't realize that I am the Son of David. David had to wear those name tags, and I will not write him off, for I have forgiven him."

MacDonald further imagines Jesus going to the water to present Himself to John. The Savior is baptized. When He comes up, all of the ink has been washed away and is going down the river.

That's what Jesus' ministry is all about. Without Him, you and I drown.[7]

It's that simple. So, what is your decision?

1. Pamela Paul, "The Power of Uplift," *Time,* January 17, 2005.

2. Josh Ulick, "Why Religion Helps," *Newsweek,* November 10, 2003, 47.

3. "A Major Life of Saint Francis," *Christianity Today,* vol. 31, no. 14.

4. David Neff, "The Passion of Mel Gibson," *Christianity Today,* March 2004.

5. Bipasha Ray, "Exhibit Recalls 1919 Boston Molasses Flood," *AOL News,* January 23, 2004, quoted in Amy McNelly "Last Will and Testament," April 13, 2008, http://idisk.mac.com/pullmanpc-Public/Sermons/2008/041308.pdf.

6. Stuart Briscoe, "Christmas 365 Days a Year," *Preaching Today,* tape no. 135.

7. Gordon MacDonald, "Repentance," *Preaching Today,* tape no. 121.

Chapter 12

SUMMARY

---

1 Peter

Carmaker Lee Iacocca reflects, "Here I am in the twilight years of my life, still wondering what it's all about. I [know] this: fame and fortune is for the birds."[1] Actor Orlando Bloom says, "Tell me what [life's] all about, because I'd love to know. Money and power aren't what life is about."[2]

Gary Carter was inducted into Major League Baseball's Hall of Fame on July 27, 2003. In his acceptance speech, he shared his answer to the question "What's it all about?"

> Above all I want to thank my Lord and Savior Jesus Christ. A great verse that spoke to me while I was writing my speech and kind of explains what it's all about comes from Psalm 118. "I love you, Lord; you are my strength. The Lord is my rock, my fortress and my savior. My God is my rock in whom I find protection. He is my shield, the strength of my salvation and my stronghold. I will call on the Lord who is worthy of praise" (Psalm 118:1–3 NLT).
>
> I praise the Lord my God, my best friend, for giving me the ability, the desire, the love, and the guidance that has brought me here today. Without You, I would be nothing.[3]

When exploring the question, "What's it all about?" this great baseball legend lifted his eyes toward heaven and proclaimed, "It is God—my rock . . . my shield, the strength of my salvation and my stronghold." Only in God do we discover what life is *really* all about.

In studying Peter's first letter we have heard the apostle ponder that question, "What's it all about?" Three major themes have emerged in his answer. Before we consider Peter's second letter, let's review these themes.

SANCTIFICATION

First, Peter has emphasized sanctification—this supernatural process of growing into the likeness of Jesus. Peter describes this miracle of sanctification as the natural response to the salvation that we receive in Christ. "As obedient children, do not conform to the evil desires you had when you lived in ignorance. But just as he who called you is holy, so be holy in all you do; for it is written: 'Be holy, because I am holy' " (1 Peter 1:14–16).

We are called to grow in holiness, that is, into the likeness of God. We are called to be sanctified, which means we grow up and become like Christ. Again, listen to Peter, "Therefore, rid yourselves of all malice and all deceit, hypocrisy, envy, and slander of every kind. Like newborn babies, crave pure spiritual milk, so that by it you may grow up in your salvation, now that you have tasted that the Lord is good" (1 Peter 2:1–3).

Max Lucado likens this process of sanctification to the time their family got a dog. He writes:

> We discovered a woman in South Carolina who breeds golden retrievers in a Christian environment. From birth the dogs are surrounded by inspirational music and prayers. (No, I don't know if they tithe with dog biscuits.) When the trainer told me that she had read my books, I got on board. A woman with such good taste is bound to be a good breeder, right?
>
> So we ordered a pup. We mailed the check, selected the name Molly, and cleared a corner for her dog pillow. The dog hadn't even been born, and she was named, claimed, and given a place in the house.
>
> Can't the same be said about you? Long before your first whimper, your Master claimed you, named you, and hung a reserved sign on your room. You and Molly have more in common than odor and eating habits. (Just teasing.)
>
> You're both being groomed for a trip. We prefer the terms *maturation* and *sanctification* to *weaning* and *training,* but it's all the same. You're being prepared for your Master's house. You don't know the departure date or flight number, but you can bet your puppy chow that you'll be seeing your Owner someday.[4]

Peter speaks often of the glorious day when Christ will come again. As we wait, he challenges us to grow in grace, to participate in the adventure of sanctification.

SUFFERING

The second major theme in 1 Peter is suffering. Over and over the apostle encourages Christians to live above reproach when suffering. "If you should suffer for what is right," Peter writes in chapter 3, verse 14, "you are blessed."

Later, in chapter 4, Peter writes,

> Dear friends, do not be surprised at the painful trial you are suffering, as though something strange were happening to you. But rejoice that you participate in the sufferings of Christ, so that you may be overjoyed when his glory is revealed. If you are insulted because of the name of Christ, you are blessed, for the Spirit of glory and of God rests on you. If you suffer, it should not be as a murderer or thief or any other kind of criminal, or even as a meddler. However, if you suffer as a Christian, do not be ashamed, but praise God that you bear that name. . . . So then, those who suffer according to God's will should commit themselves to their faithful Creator and continue to do good (verses 12–19).

Indeed, suffering can help us to grow. Suffering can be like a fertilizer for sanctification. Henry Cloud and John Townsend, in their book *How People Grow,* explain how God uses suffering to stretch our souls to grow into something stronger. Like Peter, Cloud and Townsend make a distinction between good pain and bad pain.

They illustrate it like this: Suppose you're walking in an alley at night and a masked man approaches you, stabs you in the stomach, takes all your money, and leaves you in an unconscious state. You'd call that man a mugger.

Now imagine that you drive to the local hospital. Again, a masked man approaches you, only this time you're in a brightly lit room. Using a knife, he cuts your stomach open, takes all your money, and leaves you in an unconscious state. You'd call him a doctor.

The first scenario is a mugging; the second is a surgery. Both cause pain.[5]

But there is good pain and bad pain, just as there is redemptive suffering and there is destructive suffering. On the one hand, redemptive suffering presses us to the breaking point where we must go in order to grow and find healing. During those difficult times we learn to press on—to push through the fear, the trials, the pain, in order to experience maturity, completion, and sanctification. Peter also points out that redemptive suffering is a powerful witness to nonbelievers. Like going through surgery, the benefits of redemptive suffering outweigh the trauma involved.

On the other hand, destructive suffering is wasted suffering. It comes from falling into patterns of sin and avoiding the positive pain of growth. Often it is the consequence of rebelling against God, and it results in great pain. It's a mugging of one's soul. Peter warns us to avoid this kind of pain by living a Christ-centered life.

SACRIFICE

A third and final theme that we will highlight from 1 Peter is sacrifice. Peter speaks freely, and often, of the ultimate sacrifice of Christ on the cross. He also calls us to model that same spirit of sacrifice through voluntary selflessness, or submission. He speaks directly to husbands and wives, to masters and slaves, to the young and the old, calling all of us to lead lives of submission or sacrifice.

The ultimate symbol of sacrifice, of course, is the cross. Really, *that's* what it's all about.

A story comes to mind from Peggy Noonan's book *When Character Was King*. She tells of a story that the Russian president Vladimir Putin once shared with President George W. Bush.

When Putin was young, his mother gave him a cross to wear around his neck. At first he hid it in a jewelry box, but he eventually started wearing it. He even had it blessed while on a trip to Jerusalem. It became a treasured symbol of his mother's love and her faith.

Following a house fire, the cross was missing. Putin was distressed about this so he ordered an employee to sift through the charred remains of the building in search of it. Later, the employee reported to Putin and held out a closed hand. He opened it and revealed the prized cross.

After sharing this story, Putin said to Bush, "It was as if something meant for me to have the cross."

President Bush replied, "Mr. Putin, that's what it's all about—that's THE story of the cross."[6]

I would agree with the former president, "That's what it's all about—the cross of Jesus Christ."

Live in the shadow of that cross. Revel in the sacrifice our Redeemer has made for you. See all of your suffering in the light of His suffering. And may you grow into the character of Calvary.

1. Os Guinness, *Long Journey Home: A Guide to Your Search for the Meaning of Life* (Colorado Springs, Colo.: Waterbrook Press; New York: Doubleday, 2001).

2. Neil Strauss, "Chasing Orlando," *Rolling Stone* magazine, May 19, 2005, 46.

3. Gary Carter, MLB.com, http://newyork.mets.mlb.com/NASApp/mlb/mlb/events/hof/y2003/index.jsp (accessed March 10, 2010).

4. Max Lucado, *Traveling Light: Releasing the Burdens You Were Never Intended to Bear* (Nashville, Tenn.: W Publishing Group, 2001).

5. Henry Cloud and John Townsend, *How People Grow* (Grand Rapids, Mich.: Zondervan, 2004), 207.

6. Peggy Noonan, *When Character Was King* (New York: Penguin Viking, 2001).

SECTION 2

2 PETER: KEEP ON, CHRISTIANS

Chapter 13

KEEP ON

2 Peter 1:1, 2

Whether you like the Rocky movies or not, you can't deny the films have been wildly successful. *Rocky,* made for a measly $1.2 million and shot in only twenty-eight days, was a mega hit; it made more than $117 million, won three Oscars, including Best Picture, and spawned five sequels, *Rocky II, III, IV, V,* and *Rocky Balboa*—with talk of still another sequel!

So how do you explain the timeless appeal of Rocky? I suspect that what we admire most about this fictitious boxer is his keep-on attitude. He was beaten and battered and bloodied, but the man just didn't know how to quit.

We're inspired by this never-say-stop, do-or-die, keep-on spirit of Rocky, aren't we? It is this same spirit that Peter calls Christians to manifest in their lives.

We can summarize the message of 2 Peter in two words: "Keep on!" In his first letter, Peter shares words of comfort and encouragement with believers who were being attacked externally. Christians were suffering under the cruel tyranny of the insane emperor Nero. Three years later Peter wrote a final letter to the church. Of course the believers were still being persecuted, so the second letter rings with a tone of encouragement as did the first. But in the second letter, Peter warns Christians of internal threats to the church, such as complacency and heresy.

In this second letter from Peter, a number of additional themes emerge, such as diligence, hope, and warnings against false teachers. Foundational to these themes, however, is the overarching message that Peter has for the church to "keep on." This message is just as relevant today. We must keep on and remain faithful to Jesus.

With that overview in mind, consider the first couple verses of 2 Peter, "Simon Peter, a servant and apostle of Jesus Christ, to those who through the righteousness of our God and Savior Jesus Christ have received a faith as precious as ours: Grace and peace be yours in abundance through the knowledge of God and of Jesus our Lord" (2 Peter 1:1, 2).

Peter begins by identifying himself first as a servant of Jesus Christ; second, he identifies himself as an apostle. This order is not accidental. Peter makes it clear that first and foremost, he is a servant of Jesus. In 1 Peter 5:1–4, Peter shared the basic principles of servant leadership that he learned from Jesus. Now as he nears his own death, Peter humbly acknowledges his dependence upon his Master, Jesus Christ.

Still today, Jesus is looking for servants who have that kind of uncompromising devotion to Him. John Kenneth Galbraith, in his autobiography, *A Life in Our Times,* provides a snapshot of that kind of devotion. It had been a wearying day, and Galbraith asked Emily Gloria Wilson, his family's housekeeper, to hold all telephone calls while he took a nap. Shortly thereafter the phone rang. Lyndon Johnson was calling from the White House. "Get me Ken Galbraith. This is Lyndon Johnson."

"He is sleeping, Mr. President. He said not to disturb him."

"Well, wake him up. I want to talk to him."

"No, Mr. President. I work for him, not you."

Galbraith writes, "When I called the President back, he could scarcely control his pleasure. 'Tell that woman I want her here in the White House,' " the president said.[1]

Peter grew from a deny-the-Lord-three-times kind of follower into this Emily Wilson kind of devotee. We see this servant's spirit in the greeting in which Peter refers to himself first of all as a servant of Jesus Christ.

Notice that Peter identifies the recipients of his letter, "To those who through the righteousness of our God and Savior Jesus Christ have received a faith as precious as ours" (2 Peter 1:1).

William Barclay offers insightful commentary on the audience that Peter is addressing. Barclay writes:

> Peter puts this very vividly, using a word which would at once strike an answering chord in the minds of those who heard. Their faith is *equal in honour and privilege.* The Greek is *isotimos; isos* means

"equal" and *timo* means "honour." This word was particularly used in connection with foreigners who in a city were given equal citizenship with the native citizens. Josephus, for instance, says that in Antioch the Jews were made *isotimoi,* "equal in honour and privilege," with the Macedonians and the Greeks who lived there. So Peter addresses his letter to those who had once been despised Gentiles but who had been given equal rights of citizenship with the Jews and even with the apostles themselves in the kingdom of God.[2]

Isn't it good news, friend, how God accepts all of us? Jew or Gentile, black or white, good or bad, rich or poor—God includes every one of us as His beloved children. So it is that Peter's letter of encouragement and good news is addressed to each one of us. There is no higher priority to our heavenly Father than you and me, His children.

Sitting in the Columbus, Ohio, airport I was practicing my primary spiritual gift—eavesdropping. Close by, a conversation between a father and his son (who I guessed was four or five) carried to me loud and clear.

"Woooooowie Voom! Daddy! Look at that one," the boy marveled, pointing at a jet taxiing on the tarmac. "Whoa! Look at that one, Daddy!" He pointed the opposite direction at a DC-10.

The son paused for a moment, then said, "Daddy, when I be growed up, more than anything in the world I want to drive one of those jets. Can I, Daddy? Please, Daddy?"

"Sure, son, you can be a pilot if you want to. You'll have to read a lot of books."

"I will, Daddy. Because more than anything I want to be jet driver when I be a grown-up."

The boy kept gawking at the airplanes, then looked at his dad and asked, "Daddy, when you was my age, what did you want to grow up to be?"

I loved the father's answer. His response sent me scrambling through my luggage to record it in my journal.

The father looked to his son and said, "When I was your age, more than anything in the world, I wanted to grow up to become . . . your daddy."

Our heavenly Father responds in the same tender way to us. His dream job is to be our Father. To Him we are most important. His feelings about us have nothing to do with what we do or how we behave. His love is not conditional on whether or not we pay tithe. Or go to church. Or eat tofu.

We are unconditionally loved by God. According to Peter, we enjoy "equal rights of citizenship . . . even with the apostles themselves in the kingdom of God."

Peter then concludes his greeting, "Grace and peace be yours in abundance through the knowledge of God and of Jesus our Lord" (verse 2).

In his introductory comments, Peter makes it clear that "grace and peace" can be ours—"in abundance." Grace and peace are descriptors of kingdom life. It's possible to live this rich, abundant life that is marked by grace and peace. As we will read in 2 Peter, this life is very desirable; it's a life of grace, peace, kindness, goodness, self-control, perseverance, godliness, and love. In short, it's living "on earth, as it is in heaven," as Jesus prayed for in the Lord's Prayer.

How encouraging this letter must have been for the Christians in the first century. Still today, Peter's words bring hope and comfort to those of us who claim the name of Christ in a world that is openly rebellious to God.

"Keep growing in grace and peace," Peter encourages us. No matter how difficult life may become, God is with you. He understands the pain and hardship of the human race. He went to the cross for you and me. He was beaten. He was battered. He was bloodied. But He just wouldn't quit.

One day, He turned to His follower, Simon, and He said, "Simon, you know the Spirit that has been in Me—I'm going to put that Spirit in you. To mark this moment, I'm going to give you a new name, the name Peter."

Do you know what his name means? The Greek word is *petros*. It means "rock"—Jesus renamed him "Rock" or "Rocky." Old Rocky would make a lot of mistakes—he would take his eyes off Jesus and nearly drown; he would deny that he even knew his Lord. But his Lord would not give up on him. So Rocky scraped himself up off the mat, and he kept fighting the good fight.

Then just before he was martyred for the cause of Christ, he sat down and wrote one final letter. And in the letter he invited other followers of this Jesus to sell out to the kingdom and experience this more-abundant life. In that letter he would exhort fellow believers to keep on. Keep on believing. Keep on fighting the good fight. Keep on growing. And if you do, Peter assures us, some day soon you will be as triumphant as Rocky.

---

1. *Reader's Digest,* December, 1981, http://www.sermonillustrations.com/a-z/s/servant .htm (accessed March 10, 2010).

2. William Barclay, *The Letters of James and Peter,* rev. ed. (Philadelphia, Pa.: Westminster Press, 1976), 291.

Chapter 14

KEEP ON GROWING

---

2 Peter 1:3—9

When guests visit your home, what do they notice? According to the November 2006 issue of *Good Housekeeping* magazine, guests are inclined to notice a lot. First, they spy piles of mail lying around. Second, they notice dust and cobwebs. Third, they notice a messy bathroom. Fourth, they notice dishes in the sink. And finally, our guests notice full trash cans. Like it or not, people make judgments about us based on our homes.[1]

Similarly, like it or not, people make judgments about us based on what they see in our lives. So ask yourself: When people look at me, what do they see? Do they see me as the average person pursuing the values of the world? Or do they see in me the character of Christ? That is, someone pursuing the values of God's kingdom?

Continuing in 2 Peter, we hear the apostle urging us to keep on growing in godliness. Peter writes, "His divine power has given us everything we need for life and godliness through our knowledge of him who called us by his own glory and goodness" (2 Peter 1:3).

Peter begins his second letter by urging us to grow in God. He starts by identifying how that happens—it is only through God's "divine power" that we experience "life and godliness." The power to grow doesn't come from within us, but from God. Growing spiritually in our own power is as absurd as trying to grow taller in our own power.

David Pollack tried to grow taller in his own power. His attempt was unsuccessful. The *USA Today* carried a quote by the defensive end on the University of Georgia football team. Pollack said he would do anything to

100

make himself taller. He said, "I've been sleeping upside down. It's not working."[2]

Well you don't grow taller by sleeping upside down. Growth doesn't happen by trying harder. And you don't grow spiritually by trying harder. No, there is a "divine power" at work that outfits us for "life and godliness." It's the work of the Spirit, from the inside out, that produces growth. Peter contends that it is through God's "glory and goodness" that we grow.

Back to the text: "Through these"—that is, through God's glory and goodness—"he has given us his very great and precious promises, so that through them you may participate in the divine nature and escape the corruption in the world caused by evil desires" (verse 4).

It is possible to participate in the divine nature of God and escape "the corruption in the world caused by evil desires." God's Word assures us that we can escape the corruption of the world. This is good news, for as enticing as this world is, the inevitable result is death.

Joe Gutierrez provides us a picture of this. In his book *The Heat: Steelworkers' Lives and Legend*, he tells of his forty-two years working in the steel industry. In one story, called "Snow Danced in August," he describes a scene of silvery dust flakes that frequently floated to the floor in an area of the mill where steel strips rolled over pads in a tall cooling tower. Workers and visitors alike flocked to this dramatic sight, which was especially picturesque at night.

The dust, however, was asbestos. "Everybody breathed it," writes Gutierrez. He now suffers from the slow, choking grip of asbestosis, as do many of his colleagues. He writes, "Can't walk too far now. I get tired real fast and it hurts when I breathe, sometimes. And to think we used to fight over that job."

How many things in our culture resemble the silver flakes in that steel mill? Enticing—but deadly.[3]

Why would anyone sell out to the value system of this world? Sure it looks good, but it results in death.

Peter assures us that we can escape the deadly effects of sin. How? Through the "divine nature" of Jesus Christ, living in us.

In the following verses, Peter describes a better way to do life—by living according to the values of God's kingdom. This is an adventure of life and godliness and spiritual growth. Listen to his guidance:

> For this very reason, make every effort to add to your faith goodness; and to goodness, knowledge; and to knowledge, self-control; and

to self-control, perseverance; and to perseverance, godliness; and to godliness, brotherly kindness; and to brotherly kindness, love. For if you possess these qualities in increasing measure, they will keep you from being ineffective and unproductive in your knowledge of our Lord Jesus Christ. But if anyone does not have them, he is nearsighted and blind, and has forgotten that he has been cleansed from his past sins (verses 5–9).

Here, Peter shows us a picture of what we aspire to be as followers of Christ. These are the marks of a fully devoted disciple of Jesus: faith, goodness, knowledge, self-control, perseverance, godliness, brotherly kindness, and love. These are the characteristics that define the authentic Christian. If you don't notice these virtues in someone, then that person is not a true follower of Christ.

For example, consider the story of Dennis, from Katy, Texas. Dennis needed to get a suit cleaned before he left on a trip. He drove across town to a business displaying a huge sign, "One-Hour Dry Cleaners."

After filling out the paperwork, he said to the woman behind the counter, "I'll be back in an hour to pick this up."

She said, "I can't get this back to you until next week."

Dennis was confused. Pointing to the neon sign out front, he said, "I thought you did dry cleaning in an hour."

"Oh no," the woman explained. "That's just the name of the store—One-Hour Dry Cleaners."

Those of us who claim the name of Christ, but fail to act like the One whose name we bear, create confusion and disillusionment for those who have yet to believe.

Peter reminds us of how true believers behave. They act in faith, goodness, knowledge, love, and so on. Peter tells us to "make every effort" to grow in these virtues of the Spirit. Our effort, however, does not happen by gritting our teeth and clenching our fists to try harder. Our effort must always be invested in knowing Jesus. By living in the presence of Jesus, we are transformed into His likeness.

Keep in mind the reflection of D. A. Carson:

People do not drift toward holiness. Apart from grace-driven effort, people do not gravitate toward godliness, prayer, obedience to Scripture, faith, and delight in the Lord.

We drift toward compromise and call it tolerance; we drift toward disobedience and call it freedom; we drift toward superstition and call it faith. We cherish the indiscipline of lost self-control and call it relaxation; we slouch toward prayerlessness and delude ourselves into thinking we have escaped legalism; we slide toward godlessness and convince ourselves we have been liberated.[4]

Peter goes on to describe these attributes of God by explaining that as we manifest these fruits of the Spirit we begin to taste kingdom life. We experience the rich blessings and unparalleled freedom of life with God. Listen to Peter's description, "Therefore, my brothers, be all the more eager to make your calling and election sure. For if you do these things, you will never fall, and you will receive a rich welcome into the eternal kingdom of our Lord and Savior Jesus Christ" (verses 10, 11).

The reward is out of this world. But it's not just the reward of eternal life in heaven some day; we receive benefits in the here and now. For you see, we can experience the abundant life in Christ *today!* The gospel Jesus preached was that the kingdom of God has come. We can live in the abundance of God today.

Listen to this profound observation from Dallas Willard:

The abundance of God is not passively received and does not happen to us by chance. The abundance of God is claimed and put into action by our active, intelligent pursuit of it. We must act in union with the flow of God's kingdom life that comes through our relationship with Jesus.

We cannot do this, of course, purely on our own. But we must act. Grace is contrasted with earning but not with effort. Well-directed, decisive, and sustained effort is the key to the keys of the kingdom and to the life of restful power in ministry.[5]

I want that "life of restful power," don't you? As Willard points out, this does not happen by passivity or by chance. He says, "We must act in union with the flow of God's kingdom life that comes through our relationship with Jesus." It takes "well-directed, decisive, and sustained effort."

Willard's distinction is an important one: grace is not about earning—but there *is effort* involved. We will never earn our way into God's kingdom. But we must "make every effort" to live in the reality of God's kingdom. So what does this effort entail?

Well, this kingdom life with God can be experienced through the regular, intentional practice of the spiritual disciplines. Ironically, it is through the disciplines that we experience the freedom Christ has to offer. You see, through the disciplines of prayer, Bible study, corporate worship, solitude, serving, giving, fasting, etc., we are catapulted into the presence of God. As we live moment by moment in the presence of God, His Spirit dwells in us, and we are changed into His likeness. By doing this we are not earning our salvation; rather, we are rightly channeling our efforts to live in a place of complete surrender whereby the Spirit has His way in us.

Elton Trueblood put it this way:

> We have not advanced very far in our spiritual lives if we have not encountered the basic paradox of freedom, to the effect that we are most free when we are bound. . . . The one who would like to be an athlete, but who is unwilling to discipline his body by regular exercise and by abstinence, is not free to excel on the field or the tracks. . . .
>
> With one concerted voice the giants of the devotional life apply the same principle for the whole of life with the dictum: Discipline is the price of freedom.[6]

The principle is simple: We keep on growing through the practice of the spiritual disciplines that put us in God's presence. Through this discipline, we are free! But discipline, of course, requires focus and intentionality. We can't wander aimlessly and hope to land in God's kingdom.

MARATHON STUPIDITY

An embarrassing experience comes to mind. I was in Porto Allegre, Brazil, when I decided to take an afternoon jog. I pulled on some shorts, strapped up the sneakers, and said to my dad, "I'll be back in an hour or so." I took to the streets, meandering through quiet neighborhoods and hustling business districts. Soaking in the sights, smells, and sounds of a new culture, I reveled in my idyllic afternoon. Idyllic, that is, until I tried to return to my hotel.

I took a left then a right—but nothing looked familiar. I wondered if I should have gone right then left. I searched for an hour. Two hours. Three hours. Worry paralyzed me since I had no identification, no money, no shirt, and no idea how to speak Portuguese.

A marathon later, I did something that does not come naturally to me as a guy—I asked for directions. "Excuse me, sir, do you know where the hotel is that I am staying at?"

"Vut hotel ooo stay it?" he queried in broken English.

"How would I know?" I asked. "You live here."

He glared at me as if I were a few beans short of a stuffed burrito. Because I couldn't remember the name of the hotel, nobody could help me.

It is a frightening and foolish thing to wander aimlessly. This is true in a personal sense (as I discovered in Brazil). It is also true in a spiritual sense (as you may have discovered in your life).

Nevertheless, some Christ-followers seem content to wander aimlessly. They appear to have no direction, no goals—and, consequently, no spiritual growth. For them, faith is something that is stuck into a compartment labeled "Church." And most everything else—from buying Michael Lambert's latest CD to scoring a promotion at work—overshadows a focused craving for rich, spiritual growth.

The apostle Paul agrees with Peter's emphasis on spiritual growth. He explains that a flat, ho-hum pattern of spiritual growth is unacceptable for the fully devoted disciple of Christ. Instead, Paul urges believers to "grow up in every way into him who is the head, into Christ" (Ephesians 4:15, RSV). Paul also describes how he felt the intense "pains of childbirth" until Christ would be formed in His followers (Galatians 4:19). Clearly, Christ longs to see His children grow into His likeness.

High in the Alps is a monument raised in honor of a faithful guide who perished while ascending a peak to rescue a stranded tourist. Inscribed on that memorial stone are these words: He Died Climbing. Similarly, a maturing, growing Christian should foster the same attitude, right up to the end of life. Every day should find us climbing always higher into the likeness and presence of God.

So are you growing? Are you significantly more Christlike today than you were last year? Last month? Yesterday? If not, perhaps you are aimlessly wandering—which is a frightening and foolish thing to do. And I ought to know. After all, it took me six hours to (accidentally!) find my way back to my father at the hotel in Brazil. Trust me, you don't want to do that when it comes to your Father.

1. "Five Things People Really Notice," *Good Housekeeping,* November 2006, 42.

2. David Pollack, "Quotebook," *USA Today,* April 22, 2005.

3. "Steelworkers Break the Mold," *Chicago Tribune,* June 27, 2001.

4. D. A. Carson, quoted in "Reflections," *Christianity Today,* July 31, 2000.

5. Dallas Willard, "Taking God's Keys," *Leadership,* vol. 9, no. 4, Fall 1998, 57.

6. Elton Trueblood, *The New Man for Our Time* (New York: Harper Collins, January 1970).

Chapter 15

KEEP ON REMEMBERING

---

2 Peter 1:10–15

Ellen DeGeneres once lamented her memory loss on Oprah's show, "No matter who comes up to me—they're just, like, 'I can't believe you don't remember me!' I'm like, 'Oh, Dad, I'm sorry!' "[1]

Maybe you can relate to Ellen because your memory is not as good as you'd like. As a preacher, I'm always trying to remember stories to use as illustrations in the pulpit, but my problem is that even though I have a photographic memory, I can't figure out how to take the lens cap off. So as for remembering sermon illustrations, I can relate to Mark Twain, who once said, "When I was younger, I could remember anything, whether it happened or not."[2] I suspect we've all felt that frustration of not being able to recall things we should remember.

The apostle Peter tells us that remembering is a worthwhile spiritual exercise. He writes,

> So I will always remind you of these things, even though you know them and are firmly established in the truth you now have. I think it is right to refresh your memory as long as I live in the tent of this body, because I know that I will soon put it aside, as our Lord Jesus Christ has made clear to me. And I will make every effort to see that after my departure you will always be able to remember these things (2 Peter 1:12–15).

Peter is saying here that he doesn't want believers to forget the basics of Christian faith. Knowing the basics is important in every arena.

When Jack Nicklaus was the undisputed number-one golfer in the world, he was asked how he stayed at the top. Nicklaus explained that at the end of every golf season, he returned to his first coach and asked the coach to teach him the basics of the game all over again. Every season he relearned the basic building blocks of a good golf swing. There wasn't anything new to learn; he just needed to be reminded.

Peter reminds believers that there is no new revelation to be learned. He just wants the believers to remember those truths of which they already have a settled conviction. So Peter writes, "I will always remind you of these things, even though you know them and are firmly established in the truth you now have." It's good to keep going back to the basics and remember what a successful life with God looks like.

Why is Peter so insistent about reminding them of this truth? Well in verses 13 and 14, he gives a personal reason—his death is near. Peter reveals that his time on earth is short when he says, "I think it is right to refresh your memory as long as I live in the tent of this body."

Peter refers to his body as a tent, just as Paul the tentmaker did in 2 Corinthians 5:4. The body as a tent was a popular metaphor with early Christian writers. For example, in *The Epistle to Diognetus,* we find this statement: "The . . . soul dwells in a mortal tent." William Barclay points out that this picture comes from the travels of the patriarchs in the Old Testament. They had no permanent residence but lived in tents because they were traveling to the Promised Land.

Peter goes on to say, "I know that I will soon put it aside"—that is put his tent or his earthly body aside, "as our Lord Jesus Christ has made clear to me." Peter says that Jesus Christ made it clear that his death would be soon. Peter's comment here could well be a reference to John 21:18, 19, in which Jesus predicted Peter's manner of death, " 'When you are old you will stretch out your hands, and someone else will dress you and lead you where you do not want to go.' Jesus said this to indicate the kind of death by which Peter would glorify God." Peter is now old, and he recognizes that Jesus' words about his death are about to be fulfilled.

Now notice the next verse. "And I will make every effort to see that after my departure"—or after my exodus—"you will always be able to remember these things" (2 Peter 1:15). *Exodus,* of course, is the word used to describe the departure of the children of Israel from Egypt en route to the Promised Land. Peter sees his death, not as the end but as an inevitable step in his journey toward the Promised Land.

As Peter faces his mortality, he wants the believers to remember the truth of the gospel. He urges us to instill the truth of the gospel so deeply within our souls that we can never forget it.

Alan McCann, the rector of Holy Trinity Church of Ireland, offers this commentary on the text,

> When you fall into sin what at that moment have you forgotten? It is not that at that precise moment you don't believe in God or that you don't believe the Bible. Is it not that for a moment you have forgotten the truth of the gospel? Is it not a case that you have forgotten the consequences of sin and the cost of forgiveness of sin? When we fall from grace it is not that we have become unbelievers but that we have forgotten our need of grace, the cost of that grace and the eternal consequences of sin. Peter does not want the believers of Asia Minor to forget, nor should we.[3]

So important is this calling to remember the gospel, that even though Peter explains that he knows he is about to die, he urges believers in this one thing. This is the heart of Peter's farewell message: Remember.

You know when people are at the finish line of life, aware that they are about to die, that is not a time to talk about trivial matters. On their deathbed, you won't hear many people talking about the weather or the stock market or the Red Sox. When you realize that your life is about to end—as Peter here clearly articulates is the case for him—then you're focused on what is most important in life. Deathbed conversations tend to cut through the trivia and focus on what really matters most.

Randee Rosenfeld of Egg Harbor Township in New Jersey, tells of her father's deathbed experience. On August 27, 1996, Randee's mother woke her in the middle of the night and asked her to call 9-1-1. An ambulance arrived at the house and took her father to a local hospital in South Jersey. The following evening, he went into a coma, and the doctors decided to medevac him to a hospital in Philadelphia. By the time Randee and her mom reached the hospital, her dad was already in surgery.

Twelve hours later, the doctors called the waiting room and said, "An aneurysm erupted in his brain. We don't think he'll ever wake up." When Randee was allowed to see her dad, she said, "Hi, Daddy," and at that moment he opened his eyes. The doctors raced into the room and asked him several questions. How old are you? What year is it? Who is the president?

He answered the first three questions correctly. When they asked him a fourth question, however—Where are you?—Randee's father gave a surprising answer. He said, "Harrisburg"—which, of course, was wrong.

Over the next couple of days, Randee's dad seemed to rally. But on September 4, the first day of Randee's senior year of high school, Randee was picked up early. When she reached the hospital, her mother was waiting for her. "He had a relapse," she said. "The doctors have pronounced him brain dead."

Listen now to Randee as she tells the rest of her story.

> A few minutes later, a nurse approached and asked us to sit down. She wanted to know if we had any questions. Words came out of our mouths, words that no one in our family had ever spoken before: organ donation. We knew that it could give others a chance to live, and we wanted to help. . . .
>
> About a week after the funeral, we received a letter from the Gift of Life Donor Program telling us where the recipients were from and how their recoveries were going. The list started with the liver and the kidneys. The next sentence read: "A fifty-three-year-old man with three kids received Raymond's heart. He lives in Harrisburg, Pennsylvania."
>
> Chills rushed through me and I dropped the paper. . . . I believe my father knew that he was going to die, and I also believe he knew that his heart would not die with him. Did he somehow know that it would go on living in Harrisburg?[4]

Of course, no one knows what Randee's father knew at the end of his life. I suppose at some level, however, he was cognizant that indeed his heart would go on beating and bring life to someone in need.

Peter faced his death with this same sense of urgency to assure that the heart of his message would live on to bring life to those in need. This heart, in Peter's case, was the gospel. When he realizes his end is near, he communicates with people who know the gospel. They love the gospel. They have been persecuted for the gospel. But they are fallible human beings like you and me, and they are prone to forget the gospel, to drift away from God.

So just before he dies, Peter writes a letter of encouragement to believers to say, "Remember the gospel. Remember that God came to this earth as a baby. Remember that He lived among us. Remember that He died on a cross to secure our salvation. And now we can live in the reality of that gospel. Keep on remembering!"

1. Ellen DeGeneres on *Oprah Winfrey*, 1995, quoted in Quotations Page.com, http://www.quotationspage.com/search.php3?homesearch=remember&page=3 (accessed March 11, 2010).

2. Mark Twain, quoted in http://www.quotationspage.com/search .php3?homesearch=remember&page=3 (accessed March 11, 2010).

3. Alan McCann, "Remember, Remember," Sermon Central.com, http://www .sermoncentral.com/sermon.asp?SermonID=75343 (accessed March 11, 2010).

4. "National Story Project With Paul Auster," *NPR*, http://www.npr.org/programs/ watc/storyproject/2000/000902.story.html (accessed March 11, 2010).

Chapter 16

KEEP ON TRUSTING

———

2 Peter 1:16–21

Peter De Vries, the long-time writer for *New Yorker* magazine, was raised in a conservative Christian home of the Calvinist tradition. But as an adult, De Vries abandoned the faith of his childhood and wrote brutally satiric novels about loss of faith.

For example, in his novel *The Blood of the Lamb,* De Vries tells about Don Wanderhope, the father of an eleven-year-old girl who is diagnosed with leukemia. Just when there is a glimmer of hope and she approaches remission, an infection savages her body and she dies. Wanderhope, who just bought a cake decorated with his daughter's name in frosting, leaves the hospital, goes to a church where he had spent a lot of time praying for his daughter's healing, and hurls the cake at the crucifix hanging at the front of the church. The brightly colored icing drips from Jesus' dejected face of stone.

Phillip Yancey comments, "I feel kinship with those who . . . like [Peter] De Vries, find it impossible to keep on believing in the face of apparent betrayal. I have been in a similar place at times, and I marvel that God bestowed on me an unexpected gift of faith."[1]

Have you been there? Wavering between faith and doubt? Belief and unbelief? Have you ever wondered whether faith is just a fairy tale that helps you cope when you get kicked in the throat?

Perhaps you are wrestling with similar questions of faith. If so, it may be helpful to hear Peter explain his reasons for believing. In this passage, the disciple of Jesus explains the two foundations upon which he builds his faith.

A PERSONAL EXPERIENCE WITH GOD

In 2 Peter 1:16–18, Peter identifies this first foundation for faith,

> We did not follow cleverly invented stories when we told you about the power and coming of our Lord Jesus Christ, but we were eyewitnesses of his majesty. For he received honor and glory from God the Father when the voice came to him from the Majestic Glory, saying, "This is my Son, whom I love; with him I am well pleased." We ourselves heard this voice that came from heaven when we were with him on the sacred mountain.

How do I know that the message of Jesus Christ is valid and true? Peter answers, "Because I was there. I saw the glorified Jesus with my own eyes. I heard the voice of God speak to His Son." Peter just shares his story.

It's the most compelling argument there is, is it not? I was there! How can you argue with that?

Someone may argue against the existence of God and outline airtight arguments for atheism. But when you say, "This is the difference Jesus has made in *my* life," no one can dispute that.

The reality is, we all have evidences of God's presence in our lives. In his book *The Unnecessary Pastor,* Eugene Peterson offers this picture,

> My two sons are both rock climbers, and I have listened to them plan their ascents. They spend as much or more time planning their climbs as in the actual climbing. They meticulously plot their route and then, as they climb, put in what they call "protection"—pitons hammered into small crevices in the rock face, with attached ropes that will arrest a quick descent to death. Rock climbers who fail to put in protection have short climbing careers.
>
> Our pitons or "protection" come as we remember and hold on to those times when we have experienced God's faithfulness in our lives. Every answered prayer, every victory, every storm that has been calmed by his presence is a piton which keeps us from falling, losing hope, or worse yet, losing our faith. Every piton in our life is an example of God's faithfulness to us. As we ascend in the kingdom of God, we also realize that each experience, each victory is only a piton—a stepping stone toward our ultimate goal of finishing the race and receiving the crown of glory.[2]

We all have plenty of pitons—times when we have experienced God in our lives. This is the first foundation of faith.

THE SCRIPTURES

But remember, Peter has two foundations. The second foundation for his faith is the Bible. Notice the next verses,

> And we have the word of the prophets made more certain, and you will do well to pay attention to it, as to a light shining in a dark place, until the day dawns and the morning star rises in your hearts. Above all, you must understand that no prophecy of Scripture came about by the prophet's own interpretation. For prophecy never had its origin in the will of man, but men spoke from God as they were carried along by the Holy Spirit (verses 19–21).

Peter says the Bible is like a light that shows us where to go and how to live in this world of darkness. It is trustworthy. After all, he argues, consider the prophecies of Scripture. These prophecies are not the work of some man's own interpretation. They come from God through the Holy Spirit. Build your faith on Scripture, and you will not get lost.

A story from the Sobibór Nazi concentration camp helps to illustrate. This place of death was located near the Bug River, the scenic stretch of woods that separates Poland and Russia. Historians estimate that approximately two hundred fifty thousand Jews died there.

On October 14, 1943, Jewish slaves in Sobibór stunned their captors by using their shovels and pickaxes as weapons to revolt. Of the seven hundred prisoners who participated in the attack, three hundred made it to the woods. Of those, less than on hundred are known to have survived. Most were captured by the Germans and executed.

One of the lucky escapees who survived was Thomas Blatt—or Toivi, as he was called in his native Polish tongue. Toivi was fifteen years old when his family was incarcerated at Sobibór. His parents were killed in the gas chamber; Toivi was spared for slave labor.

Toivi and two of his friends escaped into the dense forest. During the day they buried themselves and slept. At night they crawled through the thick brush.

The boys had a lot going for them—youth, energy, and the hope that freedom was near. But what they needed most they did not have—a guide, someone who could read the stars and discern north from south. As city boys, they were clueless to navigate the terrain.

After four nights of groveling through the frozen forest, the boys spotted a building silhouetted against the dark sky in the distance. Could this be a place of refuge? Hope soared in their spirits. That is, until they got a little closer and realized the building was the east tower of Sobibór concentration camp.

They had circled through the forest and landed in the same place where they had started. Disillusioned and frustrated, they turned back into the woods.

For many people today, Toivi's experience is similar to their own. They work to escape from a life without purpose. They pursue possessions, pleasures, prestige, and so on, only to discover they've come full circle—back to a prison of meaninglessness that rapes them of hope and freedom.

For this reason, God has given us a guide that points us to a life flourishing with purpose. The psalmist called it a "lamp unto my feet, and a light unto my path" (Psalm 119:105, KJV). The Holy Bible provides the direction needed to craft a life that matters.

So read it! Marinate your mind on the counsel of God. It could save you miles of misery.

Keep on trusting. There are two foundations upon which you can build your faith—your story and Scripture.

What does this look like in real life? Consider this snapshot of the former First Lady, Betty Ford. She remembers when her husband received news that he would be the president. She writes,

> We never expected to be in that position. Not only would Jerry be assuming that demanding office, he would be doing so at a time when the country was in absolute chaos.
>
> There had never been a time in our lives when we so much needed a source of strength beyond ourselves. We would be overwhelmed otherwise.[3]

Mrs. Ford describes how comforting it was when Jerry read Proverbs 3:5, 6, to her. The text says, "Trust in the LORD with all thine heart; and lean not unto thine own understanding. In all thy ways acknowledge him and he shall direct thy paths" (KJV).

Mrs. Ford continues,

When I was confronted with breast cancer that September of 1974, a month after his swearing in, those words became especially important. With them I was able to release my concerns for the outcome of my surgery. . . .

The Biblical verses were also a great source of strength for me as I underwent alcohol and prescription drug recovery in 1978. It was a difficult time, as you can imagine, but one that ultimately brought me even closer to my family. At first, of course, there was a lot of denial, a lot of soul searching. But that faith, that belief in . . . God sustains me through recovery—an ongoing process.

There are periods in life when we realize more than ever our life is not totally in our control. Being an Episcopalian, I have always looked to God. He is what I believe in.[4]

When reflecting on a storied journey of incredible ups and downs, in the end Mrs. Ford points to two things that have carried her through: the Bible and her faith experience with God. In the end, you and I can also build our lives on these same foundations.

1. Phillip Yancy, *Reaching for the Invisible God* (Grand Rapids, Mich.: Zondervan, 2000), 38.

2. Eugene Peterson and Marva Dawn, *The Unnecessary Pastor, Rediscovering the Call* (Grand Rapids, Mich.: William B. Eerdmans Publishing Co., 2000), 12.

3. Betty Ford, *The Right Words at the Right Time,* Marlo Thomas, ed. (New York: Atria Books, 2002), 104.

4. Ibid., 105.

Chapter 17

KEEP ON GUARD AGAINST FALSE TEACHERS

---

2 Peter 2:1–22

Referring to the church, Augustine of Hippo once said, "There are many sheep without, many wolves within."[1] Unfortunately, I think his observation is still true today. There are wolves that seek to destroy you—even in the church.

But are you protected from these wolves within? Peter is concerned with this question.

In his commentary on 2 Peter, Paul Cedar writes, "After establishing the basics of the Christian faith, the credibility of himself, and the prophecies of Scripture, Peter proceeds to refute the teaching of the false prophets with truth and directness. He begins by assailing the false teachings and then denounces the false teachers themselves. He assures them of their impending doom."[2]

Listen now, in Peter's own words, "But there were also false prophets among the people, just as there will be false teachers among you. They will secretly introduce destructive heresies, even denying the sovereign Lord" (2 Peter 2:1). Peter knew all about denying the Sovereign Lord. Remember his spectacular failure in the high priest's courtyard when he denied knowing Jesus? Now, he is very concerned, hoping that no one follow his example. So in describing these false teachers, Peter said,

> They will secretly introduce destructive heresies, even denying the sovereign Lord who bought them—bringing swift destruction on themselves. Many will follow their shameful ways and will bring the

way of truth into disrepute. In their greed these teachers will exploit you with stories they have made up. Their condemnation has long been hanging over them, and their destruction has not been sleeping (verses 1–3).

Notice the characteristics of false teachers. They teach heresy, deny the Lord, bring swift destruction on themselves, lead others into shameful ways, bring truth into disrepute, and, in their greed, they exploit people. "Be careful of these false teachers," Peter warns. "They can destroy you."

The December 2006 issue of *Today's Christian Woman* contained an interesting article titled "I Grew Up in a Polygamist Family." In the article, Kathy tells her story of being one of thirteen children raised by a common father and three mothers in a polygamist community in Utah. Kathy writes, "We were constantly told to 'keep sweet,' and that 'perfect obedience produces perfect faith.' Behind these sugary slogans lay the impossible duty of living in complete obedience to the Prophet."

Kathy goes on to describe this "prophet." He manifested all of these very characteristics that Peter mentions in this passage. He was a man named Leroy Johnson, and according to his radical offshoot of Mormonism, he was regarded as the earthly leader of the community and mediator between God and man.

"We called him Uncle Roy," says Kathy. "He was a feeble old man who prophesied that he would never die—that he'd become young again and be lifted up to heaven. If I kept sweet, I'd be taken with him. I looked forward to that glorious day with hope and fear."

But, of course, that day never came. Instead, Johnson passed away at the age of ninety-three, and was succeeded by a new prophet. Well as you can imagine, these events shattered Kathy's faith. In an act of rebellion, at age eighteen, she ran away with a young man named Matt. The two were married and moved to California, but Kathy found that physical distance was not enough to separate her from her former life.

"I was ashamed I grew up in polygamy," she says. "I worried people would find out about my past, so I over-indulged in drinking, smoking, and drugs in an attempt to appear worldly. My thoughts mocked me. *You're an idiot for leaving! You didn't stay sweet and obey the Prophet! You're going to hell!* I sought therapy, but couldn't express my feelings. I wanted desperately to believe in God, yet what had he ever done for me?"

After two years of marriage, Kathy and Matt divorced. Years later, she met a man named Brian at work. Brian was a Christian and stood out in Kathy's circle of friends.

What happened next is a miracle of grace. Listen again to Kathy, "We began attending church, and Brian and I spent more time together. He had a purpose to his life, a steadiness I wanted. When I told him all about my past, he shared . . . the truth of the Bible. We began praying together. God seemed real and different than I'd ever expected."

Kathy became a serious student of God's Word. Consequently, her life was changed. She testifies, "I was amazed at the simplicity of the gospel message. I cried as I realized I could come to Christ just as I was. He didn't require perfection. Sitting there talking with Brian's mom, I prayed to receive Jesus as my Savior. Several weeks later, following counseling sessions with the pastor to make sure I fully understood, I was baptized. By God's grace, I am now a woman of faith."[3]

Isn't that a marvelous story of the power of God to change the trajectory of a life? Please note, however, in Kathy's story—as is typically the case for all born-again believers—this transformation was built upon the foundation of solid teaching that was based on the Holy Bible.

It is a frightening thing to get entangled in a web of deceit spun by false teachers. So Peter warns us, "Keep on guard against teachers propagating heresy." Note the characteristics of false teachers and be vigilant. The evil one seeks to destroy you. But praise God, by His grace we can rise above false teaching and be men and women of faith!

THE CONSEQUENCE OF FALSE TEACHING

Peter goes on in this passage now to describe the consequence of false teaching. He shares three scenarios in which God acted decisively in judgment against those who followed false teaching. The three incidents include the dismissal of the fallen angels in heaven, the Flood that destroyed the antediluvians, and the fire that destroyed the people of Sodom and Gomorrah.

> For if God did not spare angels when they sinned, but sent them to hell, putting them into gloomy dungeons to be held for judgment; if he did not spare the ancient world when he brought the flood on its ungodly people, but protected Noah, a preacher of righteousness, and seven others; if he condemned the cities of Sodom and Gomorrah by burning them to ashes, and made them an example of what is going to happen to the ungodly; and if he rescued Lot, a righteous man, who

119

was distressed by the filthy lives of lawless men (for that righteous man, living among them day after day, was tormented in his righteous soul by the lawless deeds he saw and heard)—if this is so, then the Lord knows how to rescue godly men from trials and to hold the unrighteous for the day of judgment, while continuing their punishment. This is especially true of those who follow the corrupt desire of the sinful nature and despise authority (verses 4–10).

"Make no mistake," Peter warns us. "The consequence of following false teachers is ultimately death." God will not allow sin to go unrequited. So Peter references three times when God acted in judgment; but in each case God rescued those who would follow His voice rather than to be deceived by false teaching. God rescued the angels who would trust in His love. God rescued Noah and his family from the Flood. God rescued Lot and part of his family from the fire. Even though God will act in judgment if He must, He remains true to His character of love. And because He is love, He seeks first to rescue and save whoever will follow His voice.

Time magazine carried the story of former President George Herbert Walker Bush. It detailed a trip he took to the South Pacific. During World War II, Bush had been a bomber pilot and was shot down by Japanese anti-aircraft fire. The article described Bush's return to the very place where he had been rescued from his downed aircraft.

During his return visit, Bush met with a Japanese man who said he witnessed Bush's rescue back in 1944. The veteran shared that as he and his comrades were watching the rescue take place, one of his friends remarked, "Surely America will win the war if they care so much for the life of one pilot."[4]

As Christians we can have the same confidence that we will ultimately win the battle between good and evil because God cares so much about the life of every one of His children. That is why God wants us to follow teaching that is true.

Sometimes people today argue that when it comes to spiritual matters, they have many avenues of truth. You'll hear them say, "There are many ways to heaven. Your way may be through Muhammad, another way is through Confucius, or Buddha, or Jesus . . ."

Of course, that's not what Jesus taught. He never said, "I am one of many ways to heaven." No! He said, "I am *the* way, *the* truth, and *the* life" (John 14:6, NLT; emphasis added)—not one of many roads leading to life. Jesus is the only way to God.

William Barclay, in his commentary on 2 Peter, points out that the false teaching, or heresy, centered on Christ's claims. False teachers in Peter's day were saying that Christ was not, in fact, the Son of God. He was not who He claimed to be. So Peter pens this letter and ruthlessly confronts the heresy.

Keep in mind that the word *heresy,* or *hairesis* in the Greek, did not originally carry with it a negative connotation. Originally, it simply meant "to choose." It wasn't until Peter and other apostles like Paul started writing their letters that the word *heresy* began to mean something that was negative. Why the change? William Barclay answers:

> The point is that before the coming of Jesus, who is the way, the truth, and the life, there was no such thing as definitive, God-given truth. A man was presented with a number of alternatives—any one of which he was free to believe. But with the coming of Jesus, God's truth came to men and they had either to accept or to reject it. A heretic then became a man who believed what *he* wished to believe instead of accepting the truth of God which he ought to believe.[5]

Peter does not mince words when he clearly articulates that the consequence of following false teachers is the wrath of God's judgment. Follow the road of false teachers, and it will lead you to destruction and death. Conversely, if you follow the road of the one true Teacher, Jesus Christ, it will lead you to life in His kingdom.

THE IDENTITY OF FALSE TEACHERS

Next, Peter gets specific about the conduct of teachers. How can we identify false teachers? Peter explains that false teachers:

- "are not afraid to slander celestial beings" (2 Peter 2:10).
- "blaspheme in matters they do not understand" (verse 12).
- think that "pleasure is to carouse in broad daylight" (verse 13).
- "never stop sinning; they seduce the unstable; they are experts in greed—an accursed brood!" (verse 14).
- "mouth empty, boastful words and, by appealing to the lustful desires of sinful human nature, they entice people who are just escaping from those who live in error" (verse 18).

In other words, Peter makes it clear that the conduct of false teachers gives them away. If a teacher's lifestyle is incongruent with the message he or she is teaching, then beware.

Peter concludes the chapter with a condemnation of teachers who once knew the truth but opted to teach heresy instead.

> If they have escaped the corruption of the world by knowing our Lord and Savior Jesus Christ and are again entangled in it and overcome, they are worse off at the end than they were at the beginning. It would have been better for them not to have known the way of righteousness, than to have known it and then to turn their backs on the sacred command that was passed on to them. Of them the proverbs are true: "A dog returns to its vomit," and, "A sow that is washed goes back to her wallowing in the mud" (verses 20–22).

A dog returning to vomit and hog wallowing in mud—that's vivid imagery isn't it? Matthew Henry offers this commentary, "How apt sinners are to relapse into [sin]. As the dog, after he has gained ease by vomiting that which burdened his stomach, yet goes and licks it up again, so sinners, who have been convinced only and not converted, return to sin again, forgetting how sick it made them."[6]

Henry's phrase "convinced only and not converted" is a good description of the teachers that Peter warned us about. They had been exposed to truth, perhaps they were even convinced, but not converted. Consequently, Peter had a harsh word of condemnation for them.

In the end, we must build our lives on sound teaching. After all, how we live inevitably flows out of what we believe. And what we believe is the result of what we are taught.

I think of the story out of Uganda a few years ago. *New York Times* reported of a church in Uganda that taught how the world was going to end by December 31, 2000. The teachers in that church warned the people to get ready.

So they gathered the congregation—235 people—in their church and locked the doors. Then they set it on fire. Just imagine, 235 people—including a large number of children—burned to death in a mass suicide inside a church. Why did this catastrophe happen? It was the result of false beliefs that came from false teaching.

You see, if people's minds and hearts are not being formed by right teaching and learning from Scripture, they will believe wrong things. And the inevitable end of erroneous teaching is destruction and death.

Now we need to get really personal and ask ourselves some pointed questions.

- Am I building my life on sound teaching?
- Do I honestly believe that, if I follow the teaching of Jesus, I will experience the richest, most abundant life possible?
- Who are the false teachers in my life?
- What are the TV programs I watch, and the songs I listen to, the conversations I have, and the books I read—what are these influences teaching me about God and His kingdom?
- Am I willing to intentionally shape my mind upon the teachings of Jesus? If so, what does that mean for me today?

What we are taught inevitably shapes what we believe. And what we believe inevitably shapes how we behave. In other words, our behaviors flow out of beliefs, which flow out of what we are taught. So be very careful. Keep on guard against false teachers.

1. Augustine of Hippo, *Tractates on the Gospel of John,* tractate 45.

2. Paul A. Cedar, *The Communicator's Commentary,* vol. 11, ed. Lloyd J. Ogilvie (Waco, Tex.: Word Books, 1984), 219.

3. Jan Brown, "I Grew Up in a Polygamist Family," *Today's Christian Woman,* November/December 2006, 64–67.

4. Hugh Sidney, "One Bush's War and Remembrance," September 15, 2002, http://www.time.com/time/printout/0,8816,351225,00.html#.

5. William Barclay, *The Letters of James and Peter,* The Daily Study Bible Series (Philadelphia, Pa.: The Westminster Press, 1975), 316, 317.

6. *Matthew Henry's Commentary on the Whole Bible,* new modern ed., electronic database, Hendricksons Publishers Inc., 1991.

Chapter 18

KEEP ON BELIEVING

---

2 Peter 3:1–7

Many consider it the single greatest upset in the history of sports. On September 27, 2000, twenty-nine-year-old Rulon Gardner, who grew up on a Wyoming dairy farm, walked into the Exhibition Hall in Sydney, Australia. That's when the "Miracle on the Mat" happened—he pocketed a gold medal after defeating the world's greatest wrestler of all time, Russian Alexandre Karelin.

According to legend, the Russian once carried a refrigerator home from the store and up seven flights of stairs. For thirteen years, this Russian had never lost a competition. He'd never even been scored on in ten years! Karelin was considered the most intimidating athlete in Olympic history, so feared by opponents that two prior finalists essentially quit on the mat rather than to endure the pounding.

So no one expected the American to win. In fact, the Olympic Committee chairman showed up at the match in order to present the Russian his fourth gold medal—the medal he wouldn't get.

After the historic match, reporters asked Gardner, "What was your strategy?"

Gardner explained that he approached the match with only two things on his mind, "Stay focused and hang on." And for nine excruciating minutes, Gardner said he thought only about these two things, "staying focused and hanging on."

When you think about it, Gardner's strategy is a good one that extends beyond the wrestling mat. After all, it's easy to lose our focus and give up in the spiritual battle that we all must fight—but if we stay focused and hang on, we are assured victory.

The apostle Peter has been encouraging us with the same strategy. "Dear friends, this is now my second letter to you. I have written both of them as reminders to stimulate you to wholesome thinking" (2 Peter 3:1). First, Peter reminds us that he has written these two letters as a reminder to stay focused. We must keep our minds always focused on what he labels here as "wholesome thinking." He calls us to concentrate on kingdom life. Stay focused.

He then says, "I want you to recall the words spoken in the past by the holy prophets and the command given by our Lord and Savior through your apostles" (verse 2). Here, Peter reminds us to "hang on." Hang on to the sure prophecies of the holy prophets and the teachings of Jesus. "Don't lose faith," Peter urges. This, of course, has been a theme we have noted throughout this study. Over and over we have been encouraged by Peter's challenge to keep on. "Stay focused," he says, "and hang on."

Peter elaborates in the next paragraph. Notice how he emphasizes his point by saying "you *must* understand" (verse 3; emphasis added). "First of all, you must understand that in the last days scoffers will come, scoffing and following their own evil desires. They will say, 'Where is this "coming" he promised? Ever since our fathers died, everything goes on as it has since the beginning of creation' " (verses 3–5).

Peter cites the scoffers of his day who claim that Jesus is never coming back. As an Adventist (i.e., one who believes in the, second advent of Christ), I can tell you that there is nothing new in the skeptics' question. Still today cynics chide, "Where is this 'coming' that Jesus promised? You preach about it, but when will Jesus come? Why this long delay?"

This mockery that Christians have endured through the ages is something like John Mason endured. Do you remember John Mason? If I give you two words as a hint, you'll probably remember the news story well. Here's your hint: "runaway bride." John Mason was the poor groom that was left standing at the altar all alone.

Now you remember the story, don't you? On April 30, 2005, Jennifer Wilbanks was scheduled to marry John Mason in front of six hundred guests and twenty-eight attendants. Instead, she disappeared, claiming that she had been kidnapped and assaulted by a Hispanic male and a white woman.

But when investigators began interrogating her, Jennifer confessed to fabricating the whole story. In a statement to the media, she said,

> I cannot explain fully what happened to me last week. I had a host of compelling issues which seemed out of control—issues for which I was unable to address or confine. Please, may I assure you that my running away had nothing to do with "cold feet," nor was it ever about leaving John. . . .
>
> I am truly sorry for the troubles I caused, and I offer my deep and sincere apology. I ask for John's forgiveness and that of his family. I also ask for forgiveness of my family, our friends, our respective churches, our communities, and any others I may have offended unintentionally. . . .
>
> As John said on countless occasions recently, may we follow the teaching of Scripture, in being kind to one another, tenderhearted, forgiving, just as God in Christ forgives us. Thank you.[1]

That was her official statement. Then on May 22, 2006, *People* magazine reported that Jennifer and John had officially called off their engagement. Then in September 2006, Jennifer filed a half-million dollar lawsuit against her ex-fiancé, John, for selling their story. Eventually, both parties dropped their respective suits.

Meanwhile, many marketers tried to cash in on her story. Jennifer has inspired a "runaway bride" action figure. There is a hot sauce in her honor called "Jennifer's High Tailin' Hot Sauce." An auction on eBay for a slice of toast carved with a likeness of Wilbanks closed with a winning bid of $15,400!

Now when the story broke, many people felt for dear John. Late-night comedians skewered him. Reporters harrassed him. Authorities interrogated him. Overnight, John Mason became known to the world as the "loser who got stood up at the altar."

Some would use the same label for Christians. After all, we have been waiting for millennia for our Bridegroom to show up. "I will come back" Jesus promised in John 14:3, but where is He? Why the delay?

Evangelist Ken Cox explains, "The Lord is merciful, and I think the delay has been because of mercy. I do believe there is a limit, and His mercy won't go beyond that. But by delaying His coming, He's giving more people the opportunity to be saved."

Jesus is anxious to end the delay. He longs to be united with His bride, the church. But He will not rush His return. He waits patiently for every person to have an opportunity to respond to His love.

Until that day, however, Peter reminds us that we must hang on. Keep watch. Refuse to despair. It will happen.

Ellen White reminds us, "One of the most solemn and yet most glorious truths revealed in the Bible is that of Christ's second coming, to complete the great work of redemption. To God's pilgrim people, so long left to sojourn in the 'region and shadow of death,' a precious, joy-inspiring hope is given in the promise of His appearing. . . . The doctrine of the second advent is the very key-note of the sacred Scriptures."[2]

Peter goes on then in this passage to confront the critics by explaining God's mastery over time. In 2 Peter 3:5 he writes, "But they"—that is the skeptics—"deliberately forget that long ago by God's word the heavens existed and the earth was formed out of water and by water."

You see, God is not constrained by the dimension of time in the same way that we are. He is the Creator of the universe and knows no limits of time. Understand this: There has been a delay in the Second Coming only in terms of human time and human expectations, but God's purposes know no haste and no delay. Jesus would love to have us with Him right now.

Peter continues by making a reference to a time in history when God acted in judgment. The next verse says, "By these waters also the world of that time was deluged and destroyed" (verse 6). Notice, Peter informs us that just as God acted once in judgment by destroying the earth with water, so He will act again—only this time He will destroy the earth by fire. "By the same word the present heavens and earth are reserved for fire, being kept for the day of judgment and destruction of ungodly men" (verse 7).

Make no mistake, Jesus is coming again. He will destroy this earth with fire and establish His kingdom on this earth. Let the scoffers scoff. Let the skeptics sneer. According to His timing, Jesus *will* come again.

So are you ready for Jesus to come? William Barclay suggests, "The best way to prepare for the coming of Christ is never to forget the presence of Christ."

"There's something equally as important as *coming* to Christ," says Morris Venden. "It's *staying* with Him. And if we do, we will not be ashamed at His coming. That means that if I want to know I'm ready for His coming today, then I need an *abiding relationship* with Him. Are you in a saving relationship with Christ? If you are, then you're ready for His coming right now!"[3]

Live in the presence of Jesus. Trust in Him. Live for Him. And know that whenever Jesus comes again, He will come for you; and by His grace, you will be saved. Just stay focused and hang on.

1. The Associated Press, "Runaway Bride: 'I Cannot Fully Explain What Happened,' " *USA Today,* May 5, 2005, http://www.usatoday.com/news/nation/2005-05-05-runaway-bride_x.htm (accessed March 11, 2010).

2. Ellen White, *The Great Controversy,* 1888 ed., 299.

3. Morris Venden, *Nothing to Fear* (Nampa, Idaho: Pacific Press®, 1999), 20.

Chapter 19

KEEP ON REMEMBERING GOD'S PROMISE

---

2 Peter 3:8, 9

Valerie O'Connor, a high school student in Britton, Michigan, isn't in the habit of shoving her sixty-three-year-old grandfather out the door into the snow. But her grandpa, Okey Howard, is sure glad she did.

Why?

A February ice storm back in 2002 left many Michigan residents without power, so Valerie's grandfather borrowed a kerosene heater to keep pipes and family members from freezing.

Unfortunately, someone had put something other than kerosene in the tank. When Mr. Howard lit the heater, it exploded, spewing burning fuel all over his body.

Valerie saw her grandfather in flames, so she pushed him out the door into the snow and rolled on top of him to smother the fire. She suffered minor burns on her legs.

"I knew something had to be done," Valerie said later. "After a moment of shock, I just reacted."

Mr. Howard was severely burned but still had the presence of mind to stumble back into the house with a large extinguisher to put out the house fire before he lost everything.

Later, Mr. Howard said, "I thought I was going to die."[1]

Now I know it's not a pleasant thought, but Scripture paints a similar picture of how the world—as we know it—will end. On that day, many will die. Peter says, "The present heavens and earth are reserved for fire, being kept for the day of judgment and destruction of ungodly men" (2 Peter 3:7).

That's the bad news. The good news is that, like Okey Howard, we, too, have Someone to save us. That Someone is Jesus Christ, the Son of God who came to this earth and took upon Himself our sin. Because of His sacrifice on the cross, we can be saved from the fire that will someday destroy this earth.

The apostle continues, "But do not forget this one thing, dear friends: With the Lord a day is like a thousand years, and a thousand years are like a day" (verse 8).

Perhaps you remember the old joke of the economist who read this verse and was quite amazed; so he talked to God about it. He asked God, "Is it true that a thousand years for us is like a second to you?"

"Yes," said the Lord.

The man pressed, "Then a million dollars to us must be like one penny to you."

"Well, yes."

The man begged, "Would you please just give me one cent?"

The Lord said, "All right, I will . . . in a second."

You see, God is not constrained by the dimension of time like we are. Peter reminds us that God has mastery over time. This observation about God comes in the context of Peter encouraging Christians to hang on to the hope that Jesus is coming again—no matter what the skeptics might say.

When you wonder why the delay in the Second Coming, Peter explains that the delay is only in human terms. God is right on schedule according to His divine timetable. After all, God transcends time. To Him, a thousand years is like a second.

"Do not forget this," Peter urges. We must remember this one precious promise from God, "The Lord is not slow in keeping his promise, as some understand slowness. He is patient with you, not wanting anyone to perish, but everyone to come to repentance" (verse 9).

Why does Jesus delay His coming? Scripture informs us it's because Jesus does not want anyone to perish. Every child matters to the heavenly Father, and so He waits in the hope that "everyone will come to repentance."

An old Hasidic story tells of a great celebration in heaven after the Israelites marched through the Red Sea and the Egyptian army drowned. The angels were cheering and singing.

Then Gabriel noticed that God was conspicuously absent from the celebration. He asked the archangel, Michael, "Where is God? Why isn't God rejoicing here with us?"

Michael was puzzled, so he went in search of God. Later he returned and

Gabriel asked, "Did you find God?"

"Yes."

"So where is He?"

"God is not here," Michael explained, "because He is off by Himself weeping. You see, thousands of His children drowned today."[2]

God values *every* child. He loves Iraqis, Americans, South Africans—every child is treasured by our Father. He does not want any one to perish.

And so Jesus waits until the day, when in His timing, He will return and at last, set things right. And on that day, the scoffers will be silenced, and we will begin life with God forever.

Ellen White provides this perspective, "The Lord is coming very soon, and we are entering into scenes of calamity. Satanic agencies, though unseen, are working to destroy human life. But if our life is hid with Christ in God, we shall see of His grace and salvation."[3]

That's a comforting thought when we ponder how the world might end. There are some who wonder in fear, *Could we be tortured for our faith? Could Iran launch a nuclear attack? Could we destroy our world through global warming?*

Yes. Any of these scenarios *could* happen.

But the truth is, we don't know how the final days on earth will unfold. So if you're ever feeling queasy about the last days, then remember the words of Jesus, "Do not let your hearts be troubled. . . . I go and prepare a place for you" (John 14:1–3).

In Matthew 25, Jesus concludes a lengthy discourse about the last days by sharing three stories that tell us how to live as we wait for His return. The parable of the ten virgins reminds us to be watchful. The parable of the talents reminds us to be faithful. And the parable of the sheep and goats tells us to show mercy. Never mind the "abomination of desolations," or the "mark of the beast," or any of that other scary stuff. Just live each day with Jesus and focus on three things: Be watchful, be faithful, and show mercy. It's that simple.

Be watchful. Jesus is coming like a thief in the night. Don't be caught by surprise.

Be faithful. Read the Bible. Pray. Fast. Obey the promptings of the Spirit.

Show mercy. Call a depressed friend and just listen. Write a note of appreciation to someone. Deliver a dozen chocolate-chip cookies to the firefighters in town.

There's plenty to do while we wait for Jesus to come. Who has time to panic about how it will all end? Trust the closing chapters to God.

Stay close to Jesus. Keep on remembering, "The Lord is not slow in keeping his promise." And He did promise, "I will come back and take you to be with Me."

1. Jeff Steers, *The Exponent*, February 12, 2002.

2. Tony Campolo, *Let Me Tell You a Story* (Nashville, Tenn.: Thomas Nelson, 2000).

3. Ellen White, *Testimonies for the Church*, vol. 9 (Mountain View, Calif.: Pacific Press®, 1948), 62, 63.

Chapter 20

KEEP ON WATCHING

2 Peter 3:10–13

On February 28, 2007, the day after the Dow Jones Industrials plunged more than four hundred points, a reporter from CNN interviewed a financial expert. The reporter asked the question everyone wanted to know, "Given the violent volatility of the market, what should we do with our investments at this point? Should we buy? Sell? Or hold?"

The expert's answer struck a familiar chord for me as an Adventist. The financial analyst gave three words of advice, "Wait and watch."

Wait and watch. Don't panic. Don't buy. Don't sell. Just wait and watch.

Jesus gave the same counsel when He spoke about the chaos during the last days. "Don't panic," He said. In Matthew 24 we find an extensive list of signs that alert us to the nearness of His coming—earthquakes, wars, increase of knowledge, and so on. Jesus then trumpets the punch line in verse 42, "Therefore keep watch, because you do not know on what day your Lord will come." Then again, in Matthew 25:13, Jesus said, "Therefore keep watch, because you do not know the day or the hour."

Note, Jesus did not just say to "wait," suggesting a passive activity. Rather, He commanded, "wait and watch."

The difference between waiting and watching is illustrated by the old story of a fishing vessel returning home after many days at sea. As they neared the shore, the sailors gazed eagerly toward the dock, where a group of their loved ones had gathered. The skipper looked through his binoculars and identified some of them: "I see Bill's Mary, and there's Tom's Margaret and David's Anne."

One man became concerned because his wife wasn't there. Later, he left the boat with a heavy heart, fearing something tragic had happened to her. He hurried to his cottage. As he opened the door, she ran to meet him saying, "I've been waiting for you!"

He replied with a gentle rebuke, "Yes, but the other men's wives were waiting *and watching* for them!"

See, watching is not a spectator sport. We must be vigilant in waiting. Peter reminds us, "But the day of the Lord will come like a thief" (2 Peter 3:10). Remember that Peter was with the other disciples when Jesus said, "But understand this: If the owner of the house had known at what time of night the thief was coming, he would have kept watch and would not have let his house be broken into" (Matthew 24:43, TNIV).

Thus, Peter reminds us that the Lord will come like a thief in the night. Then he goes on to say, "The heavens will disappear with a roar" (2 Peter 3:10).

There's an interesting word picture associated with this Greek word translated "roar." The same word, *roizedon,* is used to describe the sound a spear makes as it sails through the air. The idea here is that faster than a speeding bullet, "the elements will be destroyed by fire, and the earth and everything in it will be laid bare" (verse 10).

Peter tells us that the Second Coming will catch many by surprise. So he urges us to wait and watch.

Remember, there are things we must do as we wait and watch for the soon return of our Savior. What are we to do? What kind of people should we be? Peter asks that question and then he answers,

> Since everything will be destroyed in this way, what kind of people ought you to be? You ought to live holy and godly lives as you look forward to the day of God and speed its coming. That day will bring about the destruction of the heavens by fire, and the elements will melt in the heat. But in keeping with his promise we are looking forward to a new heaven and a new earth, the home of righteousness (verses 11–13).

Here's what Peter is saying: As we *watch* for Jesus, we're called to *be* like Jesus. "Make no mistake," Peter warns us with graphic imagery, "This world will be torched and the elements will melt in the heat." But until that happens, we "ought to live holy and godly lives." Again, as we watch for Jesus, we're called to be like Jesus.

So is this even possible? Can we be like Jesus—or is the very notion like something out of a fairy tale?

Well, throughout history people have embraced fairy tales. Seems everyone wants to believe that there is something mystical and magical beyond the world as we know it.

A common theme in fairy tales suggests that an enchanted world is just a blink away. You step into a closet and you're in Narnia. You walk through the woods, and you stumble on a cottage with seven dwarfs.

But fairy tales are not only about the transformation of the world "out there." There is also an internal transformation of the characters in the stories. Frogs change into princes, ugly ducklings become swans, wooden puppets become real boys.

Frederick Buechner suggests there are similarities between the gospel and fairy tales, with one significant difference: the gospel is true.

According to the gospel, a different reality is but a blink away. You and I can live in the reality of Jesus' prayer: "on earth as it is in heaven" (Matthew 6:10). Author Ellen White reminds us that "we are fitted for heaven; for we have heaven in our hearts."[1]

We can know the joy of heaven today. Here. Now.

Pastor John Ortberg puts it this way:

> This is promised in the gospel—the good news proclaimed by Jesus: "The kingdom of God has come near; repent, and believe in the good news." The good news as Jesus preached it is that now it is possible for ordinary men and women to live in the presence and under the power of God. The good news as Jesus preached it is not about the minimal entrance requirements for getting into heaven [after] you die. It is about the glorious redemption of human life—your life.[2]

In other words, you can change. You *can* be like Jesus! Tired of the angry spirit that festers within? Or the gossip that leaks out of your lips? Or the Web sites that poison your soul? You can find a new life in Jesus! By living continually in His presence and power, you can emerge from these ingrained patterns of sin and become a new creation in Christ.

Candie's story puts flesh on the idea that transformation is possible. I met Candie in the crowded lobby of our church. She introduced herself by saying, "I want to be baptized."

"Praise the Lord," I replied. "Um, I'm sorry, I should probably know you but—"

"Oh, I'm Candie. I've been coming to your church, and I would like to become a Seventh-day Adventist."

"Great! Let's meet to talk about it."

Later that week I reviewed with her the basic doctrines of our church. She was obviously well-studied and conversant in Adventist beliefs. As part of our conversation I mentioned the concept of spiritual gifts. "For example," I said, "one of my gifts is teaching. I'm energized by talking in front of people."

"I think that's my gift too," she said.

"Really?" I tried to disguise my surprise. "Well then, um, would you be willing to say a few things at your baptism? Right before I baptize you, I'll ask you to share your testimony. Would you be comfortable with that?"

"Sure."

I never thought to ask her what her testimony was. (Ever since, I have always asked baptismal candidates to tell me their testimony first!)

Sabbath morning I stood with Candie in the baptistry. I introduced her to the church and explained that she was going to share her testimony.

Her opening words swallowed all sound in the sanctuary. "I was a teenage prostitute and worked for twelve years as a stripper."

I had never seen the members so attentive—certainly not during any of my sermons. My pulse doubled as I wondered where her story was going next.

As her story unfolded, I marveled at how poised Candie was. Her sordid saga unveiled the seediest shadows of society. Yet she spoke with confidence and candor. I readily affirmed her intuition that indeed she had a gift for public speaking. While she spared us the details of her story, she shared enough to let us know that there was a lot of brokenness and pain in her story.

"But that's all behind me now." Candie's face glowed as she spoke. "I am going to leave that old person at the bottom of this tank. God tells me that I will arise a new creation. If God's grace can cover me, then there is no such thing in God's vocabulary as an ineligible receiver. If God can change me, He can change anybody. Praise God for His incredible grace."

With that, I momentarily buried Candie in the water. Then the congregation gave her a standing ovation for what felt like fifteen minutes.

We held a potluck lunch in Candie's honor. During the meal, however, I glanced around the fellowship hall trying to spot Candie. She wasn't there. I looked in the hallway and the lobby—still no Candie.

Finally, I peaked into the worship center and saw Candie, all alone in this cavernous sanctuary sitting by the baptistry.

"Candie, are you OK?" I asked.

"Oh, Pastor, um, yeah, I'm fine."

"What are you doing in here?"

"Well, Pastor," she sighed, "I wanted to watch the water go down the drain. I can guarantee you that this baptistry will never again hold as many sins as it did today. For the first time in my life, I feel clean. Do you have any idea what that feels like? I know I am forgiven and clean. Isn't God's grace amazing?"

In that holy moment it hit me with fresh force—the power of God to forgive and transform a human life. Only God can change a prostitute into a promise-keeper. Only Christ can reconstruct the composition of a human heart. Only He can stoop into the shadows and salvage the brokenness of a spiritual casualty like Candie. Or Carl. Or Carol.

Lest you think Candie's story is any different from yours or mine, may I remind you that we all stand as moral and spiritual failures before God. It is only by His cleansing grace that we can find forgiveness and freedom from our sins.

Some day, Jesus will come and eradicate sin once and for all from this earth. What a glorious day that will be! For now, however, we wait. But remember, as we wait for Jesus, we are called to be like Jesus.

That's what Candie is doing. Fifteen years later, she is an active Seventh-day Adventist, working as a social worker to help at-risk teens. In her words, "I see so much hate and heartache in our world. I can't wait for Jesus to come! But until that day, I'll keep working in His vineyard."

---

1. Ellen White, *The Desire of Ages*, 641.

2. John Ortberg, *The Life You've Always Wanted* (Grand Rapids, Mich.: Zondervan Publishing, 2002), 28, 29.

Chapter 21

KEEP ON TRUSTING GOD

———

2 Peter 3:14–16

Alexander Maclaren writes, "The primitive church thought more about the Second Coming of Jesus Christ than about death or about heaven. The early Christians were looking not for a cleft in the ground called a grave but for a cleavage in the sky called Glory. They were watching not for the undertaker but for the uppertaker."[1]

The apostle Peter once sent a letter to these "early Christians" to encourage them to never stop looking for "the uppertaker." "So then, dear friends," he writes, "since you are looking forward to [the Second Coming], make every effort to be found spotless, blameless and at peace with him" (2 Peter 3:14).

In light of this hope that early Christians shared in the second coming of Jesus, Peter urges them to "make every effort" to be ready. You may recall this same phrase from earlier in Peter's letter (2 Peter 1:5). Here again at the end of his letter, he implores, "Make every effort . . ." Peter sandwiches his letter with the same command.

Since Peter sandwiches his letter between the same phrase, I'll follow suit and repeat Dallas Willard. Once again, here's part of his quote, "The abundance of God is not passively received. . . . The abundance of God is claimed and put into action by our active, intelligent pursuit of it. We must act in union with the flow of God's kingdom life that comes through our relationship with Jesus. We cannot do this, of course, purely on our own. But we must act. Grace is contrasted with earning but not with effort. Well-directed, decisive, and sustained effort is the key to . . . the kingdom."[2]

When Peter says, "make every effort," don't confuse that with earning

138

salvation. Salvation is free because of what Christ did on the cross. But if we covet kingdom life, or the "abundance of God" as Peter phrases it here, then it requires, in Willard's words, "Well-directed, decisive, and sustained effort."

Now I emphasize the importance of making every effort because Christians can fall victim to a state of spiritual learned helplessness. This distorted mind-set says, "The world will burn, and there's nothing I can do about it. I'm a helpless victim."

It brings to mind a video clip that shows a man and woman riding up an escalator in an empty office building. Suddenly the escalator stops, and the two riders stand there in disbelief at their catastrophic misfortune. "I don't need this; I'm already late," the woman exclaims. The man tries to bring calm to the situation by saying, "Somebody will come." Then he panics and cries out, "Anybody in there? . . . Hello!" By this point he is incredulous, "There are two people stuck on an escalator and we need help, now! Would somebody please do something?" Then the woman loses it and screams, "Heeeelp!" Her cry echoes in the building and she sighs, "I'm gonna cry."

They both just stand there stranded on the escalator, when all they'd have to do is take a few steps and they'd be free; but the easy exit never seems to cross their minds.

Peter wants to make sure that Christians do not fall victim to this kind of learned helplessness.

There *is* something we *must* be doing as we anticipate the Lord's soon return. So Peter entreats us to "make every effort" to live a holy and obedient life so that at the Second Coming we will be found "spotless, blameless and at peace with him."

So what are we to be doing as we watch for Jesus to come? We're to keep growing in Christ. Peter emphasizes this by citing the work of Paul. Take note,

> Bear in mind that our Lord's patience means salvation, just as our dear brother Paul also wrote you with the wisdom that God gave him. He writes the same way in all his letters, speaking in them of these matters. His letters contain some things that are hard to understand, which ignorant and unstable people distort, as they do the other Scriptures, to their own destruction (2 Peter 5:15, 16).

When touching on the topic of salvation, Peter references Paul, a fellow apostle. Of course, Paul wrote extensively of God's salvation. *The*

Communicator's Commentary applies Peter's reference to Paul in this way,

[Peter and Paul both] enjoyed the benefits of the salvation of the Lord, and so can we. . . .

To those who understand what Paul has written and have experienced the salvation of the Lord, it is wonderful news. But to those who continue to walk after the flesh and are untaught and unstable, they twist his teaching just as they do all of Scripture. The terrible result will be their own destruction.

What a contrast! To live in peace, without spot, blameless, and to enjoy the salvation which comes from the longsuffering of the Lord is the choice which Peter offers us as contrasted with the destruction which will come to those who twist the truth.[3]

Don't you want to live "in peace, without spot, . . . [and] enjoy the salvation which comes from the . . . Lord"? It's just a better way to live. Who wouldn't want to experience this more abundant life?

Dr. Brian McLaren's parable illustrates,

Once upon a time there was a good and kind King who had a very great kingdom with many cities. In one distant city, some people took advantage of the freedom the King gave them and started doing evil. They profited from their evil and began to fear that the King would interfere and throw them in jail. Eventually these rebels seethed with hatred for the King. They convinced the city that everyone would be better off without the King, and the city declared its independence from the kingdom.

But soon, with everyone doing whatever they wanted, disorder reigned in the city. There was violence, hatred, lying, oppression, murder, rape, slavery and fear. The King thought, *What do I do? If I take my army and conquer the city by force, the people will fight against me, and I'll have to kill many of them, and the rest will only submit through fear or intimidation and hate me and all I stand for even more. How does that really help them—to either be dead or imprisoned or secretly seething with rage? But if I leave them alone, they'll destroy each other, and it breaks my heart to think of the pain they're causing or experiencing.*

So the King did something very surprising. He took off His robes and dressed in the rags of a homeless wanderer. Incognito, He entered the city and began living in a vacant lot near a garbage dump. He took up a trade—fixing broken pottery and furniture. Whenever people came to Him, His kindness and goodness and fairness and respect were so striking that they would linger just to be in His presence. They would tell Him their fears and questions and ask His advice. He told them that the rebels had fooled them, and that the true King had a better way to live, which he exemplified and taught. One by one, then two by two, and then by the hundreds, people began to have confidence in Him and live in His way.

Their influence spread to others, and the movement grew and grew until the whole city regretted its rebellion and wanted to return to the kingdom again. But, ashamed of their horrible mistake, they were afraid to approach the King, believing that He would destroy them for their rebellion. But the King-in-disguise told them the Good News: He Himself was the King, and He loved them. He held nothing against them, and He welcomed them back into His kingdom, having accomplished by a gentle, subtle presence what never could have been accomplished through brute force.[4]

In the same way, God came to our planet to model a better way of life. By accepting Him and the sacrifice He made at Calvary, not only do we enjoy the assurance of salvation for eternity, but we also enter into this kingdom life today. Who in their right mind would reject such a scandalously good offer?

CONCLUSION

Peter concludes his letter with these words, "Therefore, dear friends, since you already know this, be on your guard so that you may not be carried away by the error of lawless men and fall from your secure position. But grow in the grace and knowledge of our Lord and Savior Jesus Christ. To him be glory both now and forever! Amen" (verses 17, 18).

His last instruction: We are called to "grow in the grace and knowledge of our Lord and Savior Jesus Christ."

That's the goal for every follower of Christ: Grow to be like Jesus. To think like Him. To love like Him. To eat like Him. To work like Him. To laugh like Him. To be like Jesus—that's the heart of spiritual life. We're called to look like Jesus. We are called to act like Jesus.

Have you ever had someone say that you look like somebody else, a celebrity perhaps? There's a Web site called MyHeritage.com that allows you to upload a head shot for a computer algorithm to analyze the image for distinct facial features. The uploaded image is then compared to a database of some twenty-five hundred celebrities and is matched against comparable famous faces, with each match being ranked by a percentile similarity score.

Recently I uploaded my picture to the Web site. I could feel my heart racing as the computer scanned my image then searched for my celebrity look-alike. The result? I have 70 percent resemblance to the politician Rudy Giuliani and 62 percent resemblance to the actor Bruce Willis.

Now what the Web site won't do is match a person's *character* to some celebrity. Most of us wouldn't want to match up to the proliferation of train-wreck relationships and grisly moral scandals.

Nobody wants the computer to report, "Since you have recently had your spouse smash in a window on your SUV with a 9-iron and your numerous affairs have gone public . . ." Or, "Since you have been pulled over for driving under the influence while uttering anti-Semitic insults, your celebrity character match is . . ." Well, you get the point.

Who cares what celebrities we look like? The real question is: *Are there sufficient character recognition points in our lives to match us, not with some celebrity, but with Christ?*

That's what Peter is driving at here at the end of his letter. He urges us to keep growing in grace.

Author Max Lucado writes,

> Growth is the goal of the Christian. Maturity is mandatory. If a child ceased to develop, the parent would be concerned, right? . . . When a Christian stops growing, help is needed. If you are the same Christian you were a few months ago, be careful. You might be wise to get a checkup. Not on your body, but on your heart. Not a physical, but a spiritual.
>
> May I suggest one? . . .[5]

Listen now, as Max gets real practical and shares the "How?" of growing in grace.

> Why don't you check your habits? . . . Make these four habits regular activities and see what happens.

First, the habit of prayer. . . . Second, the habit of study. . . . Third, the habit of giving. . . . And last of all, the habit of fellowship.[6]

I can't improve on Max's list of spiritual practices that will allow you to live in the presence of God. Through prayer, Bible study, giving, and fellowshiping, you will spend time in God's presence, and He *will* change you by allowing God to live His life in you. Then, by God's power, you will keep on growing in grace.

1. Alexander Maclaren, quoted in Edythe Draper, *Draper's Book of Quotations for the Christian World* (Wheaton, Ill.: Tyndale House Publishers, Inc., 1992), 9912–9914.

2. Dallas Willard, "Taking God's Keys," *Leadership,* Fall 1998, 57.

3. Paul A. Cedar, *The Communicator's Commentary James, 1, 2 Peter, Jude,* ed. Lloyd J. Ogilvie (Waco, Tex.: Word Books, 1984), 239.

4. Brian McClaren, *A Generous Orthodoxy* (Grand Rapids, Mich.: Zondervan/Youth Specialties, 2004), 64, 65.

5. Max Lucado and T. A. Gibbs, *Grace for the Moment: Inspirational Thoughts for Each Day of the Year* (Nashville, Tenn.: J. Countryman, 2000).

6. Ibid.

Soul Matters

In Soul Matters, with humor and wisdom
Pastor Karl Haffner points the way to
more relief for the "stressed out, worn
out, and burned out." Karl explores soul
questions, soul pain, soul community,
and soul goodness. He reminds you that
it is possible to live a sane and balanced
life in a world gone mad.
Paperback, 144 Pages
ISBN 13: 978-0-8163-2150-6
ISBN 10: 0-8163-2150-7

Paperback, 144 Pages
ISBN 13: 978-0-8163-2022-6
ISBN 10: 0-8163-2022-5

Paperback, 128 Pages
ISBN 13: 978-0-8163-1840-7
ISBN 10: 0-8163-1840-9

Paperback, 176 Pages
ISBN 13: 978-0-8163-1902-2
ISBN 10: 0-8163-1902-2

DEDICATION

Dedicated to Bev and Krystal Morris

In loving memory of Dean Morris, who came to mind often as I pored over the pages of Peter's letters. The themes of 1 and 2 Peter—the Second Coming, suffering, faith, and perseverance—fill me with hope that someday soon I'll be laughing with my friend Dean again.

SPECIAL THANKS TO

Jerry Thomas, Scott Cady, Bonnie Tyson-Flyn, and Pacific Press®—a faithful, helpful, and long-suffering publishing team.

Ken Wade, Lonnie Melashenko, and the Voice of Prophecy family—generous folk who helped to shape this book in very significant ways.

Jerry Mahn, Tasha O'Neill, Brendon Prutzman, Elliot Smith, Kay Starkey, Dan Stevens, Jerry Taylor, Chris Terry, and Clive Wilson—my colleagues who make going to work seem like a visit to Kings Island (which, on some days, is literally true).

Ted Ramirez—the best head elder in the history of church.

Fred and Mary Kaye Manchur—great friends who have so graciously introduced us to a wonderful adventure in Ohio.

Dan and Bev Cobb—some of the most generous, gracious folk alive.

Raj and Chandra Attiken—visionary leaders who inspire.

Cherié, Lindsey, Claire, and Skipper—daily reminders of how rich I truly am.

Karl Haffner

Caught Between Two Worlds

[A survival guide for end-time living]

Pacific Press® Publishing Association
Nampa, Idaho
Oshawa, Ontario, Canada
www.pacificpress.com

Cover design by Mark Bond
Cover design resources from www.Thinkstock.com
Inside design by Aaron Troia
Dedication page photo by LeAnn Yahle

The author assumes responsibility for the accuracy of all facts and quotations as cited in this book.

Unless otherwise noted all Scripture quotations are from the HOLY BIBLE, NEW IN-TERNATIONAL VERSION®. Copyright © 1973, 1978, 1984 by International Bible Society. Used by permission of Zondervan Publishing House. All rights reserved.

Scripture quotations from *The Message*. Copyright © by Eugene H. Peterson, 1993, 1994, 1995, 1996, 2000, 2001, 2002. Used by permission of NavPress Publishing Group.

Scripture quotations marked NLT are taken from the Holy Bible, New Living Transla-tion, copyright © 1996, 2004. Used by permission of Tyndale House Publishers, Inc., Wheaton, Illinois 60189. All rights reserved.

Scriptures quoted from NKJV are from The New King James Version, copyright © 1979, 1980, 1982, Thomas Nelson, Inc., Publishers.

Scriptures quoted from RSV are from the Revised Standard Version of the Bible, copy-right © 1946, 1952, 1971 by the Division of Christian Education of the National Council of the Churches of Christ in the U.S.A. Used by permission.

Scriptures quoted from KJV are from the King James Version.

Scriptures quoted from TNIV are from the HOLY BIBLE, TODAY'S NEW INTER-NATIONAL VERSION®. Copyright © 2001, 2005 by International Bible Society®. Used by permission of International Bible Society®. All rights reserved worldwide.

Additional copies of this book may be purchased online at www.adventistbookcenter.com or by calling toll-free 1-800-765-6955.

Library of Congress Cataloging-in-Publication Data:

Haffner, Karl, 1961-
  Caught between two worlds : a survival guide to end-time living / Karl
Haffner.
    p. cm.
  ISBN 13: 978-0-8163-2404-0 (pbk.)
  ISBN 10: 0-8163-2404-2 (pbk.)
  1. Bible. N.T. Peter—Criticism, interpretation, etc. I. Title.
  BS2795.52.H34 2010
  227'.9206—dc22
                                                              2010008247

10 11 12 13 14 • 5 4 3 2 1